"When I look at Joy's book, I think of Robert Kennedy's quote "tragedy is a tool for the living to gain wisdom not a guide by which to live." I think this captures the author and the players of her book in that it somehow covers hope and understanding. *Chasing My Son Across Heaven* is a selfless, raw story . . . which can perhaps bring understanding to or about tragedy."

—Honourable Lynne Yelich, MP, PC, Canada

"When someone goes through tragedy, people will often say that 'everything happens for a reason'. I've never believed or taught that. I believe that things happen with potential. Both good and bad. Tragedy has the ability to tear apart an individual, a family, a community or an entire country. But tragedy also has the ability to bring people together. And that takes choice. Joy has been the perfect example of that. She could have allowed her tragedy to destroy her. But she has rather decided to take her story and use it to help others when faced with the same pain she has gone through. That takes such courage. Meeting Joy Pavelich is one of the greatest gifts I've ever been given. I am so proud to know her and call her a friend. Anyone with the opportunity to meet her or read her book will receive the gift I did the day I met her."

—Robb Nash, The Robb Nash Project, Musician

D0645411

"There are people you meet in the world that like you to think they're qualified by way of their achievements; Joy's qualifications come from the school of hard knocks and experience. Joy is all heart and soul, and I can't think of anybody more qualified to tell the story she has so graciously decided to share with all of us. It's honest, it's painful, but it's real. It doesn't get any better than that."

—Kenny Munshaw, Singer, Songwriter, *Arms of Heaven*

"From Joy I've learned that no matter how deep the scars are, how strong the loss is, the hurt and the brokeness inside, to never stop believing or trusting or following the Path that was meant for you! And this is what she shares in *Chasing My Son Across Heaven*."

—Rui Portugal Ribeiro, Owner, Ultreia y Suseia

chasing

my son

across

heaven

A Story of Life, Loss and
the Strength of Enduring Love

V. JOY PAVELICH

RAINBOW RIDGE
BOOKS

Cover and interior design by Frame25 Productions
Cover photo © boscorelli c/o Shutterstock.com
and faestock c/o Shutterstock.com
Author photo by Danny Miller

Published by:
Rainbow Ridge Books, LLC
Virginia Beach, VA
www.rainbowridgebooks.com

If you are unable to order this book from your local bookseller, you may order directly from the distributor.

Square One Publishers, Inc.
115 Herricks Road
Garden City Park, NY 11040
(877) 900-BOOK

Library of Congress Control Number: 2019957582

ISBN 978-1-937907-66-2

10 9 8 7 6 5 4 3 2 1

Printed in India through Nutech Print Services - India

For every mother of an angel child.
Let us hold each other 'til we hold them once again.

Contents

Acknowledgments

Justin, Eric and Conner: There aren't words to describe what you three mean to me, and what the gift and grace has been in motherhood. Pain, sorrow, sadness all pale in comparison. Eric, for the love that doesn't die, I thank you. Justin and Conner, for wrapping your arms around me throughout our lives, I thank you. As we've navigated this loss over the past few years, I know we've all had to find our own way. And at times my way has tested both of you. But you've stood with me even when you couldn't understand me. Loving me when I wasn't very loveable has been the greatest gift you could give me. For your unconditional love and support, I thank you.

Family: I have been blessed with the family I was born into and that I am still a part of. My mother Carmella has been one of the most significant women in my life. I look to her daily for her advice, her wisdom. Only now am I beginning to appreciate what a gift it is to have her. Thank you, Mom, for a lifetime of caring and sharing and the foundation of love you and Dad built all of our lives upon. My two brothers, Kurt and Dallas and your families, like Mom and my boys, are the best pieces of my life. Thank you for being you. Owen and Mia, despite time and space, I love you. To my many aunts, uncles and cousins, while I don't name you, each of you are so very precious.

Friends: There are friends, and then there are friends that are family. To the Molina's; Bobby, Jenny, Michael, Jaiden and Marcus; you are an amazing gift, each of you in your own way, and I couldn't have survived this past chapter in my life story without your constant presence. To the DeBoice's; Tracey, Kevin, James and Michael (and of course Phyllis), your friendship and support continue to be a light in my life. Michelle, Ashton and Evan, sometimes friendship isn't about quantity of time, but quality of time. I haven't needed to see you to know that you are always there. Trevor, Debbie and Andrew, thank you for that lifelong connection that is as real today as when we met decades ago. The gift of forever.

I've gathered friends along the way who have each supported me in their own way, and for that I am eternally grateful. Know that you have made a difference with your friendship and love: Alwyn, Dan, Darcy, Darlene, Debby, Glen, Greg, Heather, Julie, Kathryn, Kenny, Laureen, Lesley, Lisa, Lloyd, Loreen, Margaret, Maureen, Patricia, Pam, Pam and Pam, Robb, Robin and Robin, Sheldon, Stacey and Stacey, Susan, Suzanne and Wayne. I have met many people, formed many friendships, but each of you is far more important to me than simple words can express. I hope you know that.

The Strong Women in My Life: There are two women who are both family and friend. Lynne, you've been there since I was born, and I cherish this amazing friendship we've formed that goes far beyond what our shared heritage has meant. You are a remarkable gift. Valerie, you too are someone that I cherish as I do few others in this earthly journey. Both of you are inspirations and role models that have guided me throughout my life. You need to be acknowledged as such.

Influence on This Story: Sean, for your kind offering, and the gratitude of connecting our collective pasts to this story, I thank you. Zoé, for taking up the challenge of something so difficult to comprehend, but your commitment to seeing it through the lens of a true narrative, I especially thank you. Your guidance and thoughtful intelligence brought the words of this book together in a way I couldn't have managed alone. Romie, for believing in the story and that outreach to Sean which brought him and Zoe to be such critical contributors. And finally, Margaret, you are one of the gifts Eric brought to my life and I treasure you in so many ways. Thank you for everything, including reviewing this when so many pages hurt your heart as well, and the invaluable insight you provided.

Blessings to each of you.

"It doesn't matter who you are, life, God and nature are going to challenge you—this is law. Not everyone stands tall, and not everyone survives. It isn't about what life gives you, it's about appreciating the love you have; appreciating the ones who will never leave you. Everyone will face challenges. No one ever said life would be easy. In the end, the love of family, of friends, and comradery is all we have left . . . build bridges with everyone because one bridge always leads to another."

—Eric Schmit

Eric (left), Conner (middle), and Justin (right)

Foreword

I should have known the story of Joy Pavelich and her son Eric Schmit better before I read this book. It's remarkable, really, how much I should have known, considering the similarities between my life and Joy's.

Joy and I are from almost identical ethnic backgrounds—both of our fathers' people are from the Lika region of west central Croatia—and both our families emigrated together to Canada in 1912. They were part of the great wave of European settlement on the Canadian Prairies before World War I.

Perhaps with more nostalgia than good sense, the patriarchs of our two clans selected property near present-day Kenaston, SK, which resembles the foothills and low mountains of Lika.

Known locally as the Allan Hills, they are, in places, steep and challenging for tractor driver and cattle herder alike. Not so practical for farming, but beautiful. And I can close my eyes now and place myself on a particularly lofty hill on the family's back 40 and imagine looking dozens of kilometers off to the far southern and western horizons. Perhaps Joy has a similar spot, too.

So, we were raised just a few kilometers apart, attended the same school in Kenaston, and, remarkably, after graduation both of us decided independently to go journalism school. But I was a few years older, our families didn't socialize much and, for two such similarly raised people, we didn't have much to do with each other.

That changed when I got a message last year from an old friend of mine who worked with me during my days at the CBC. Could I help a friend of hers, she asked, who'd written a new book?

The budding author, my friend went on to say, said she knew me and came from my home town. Then the remarkable story of Joy Pavelich and her son Eric, a story of which I knew nothing, came tumbling out.

I say remarkable because I found it heartbreaking, depressing, inspiring and instructive all at once.

It's a story for our times because it touches on great scourges that plague us today, including mental illness, youth suicide and the agony of dealing with Post Traumatic Stress Disorder.

Now, as a professional skeptic, a job requirement for a former CBC producer like me, meant I struggled at first with Joy's conversations in this book with her dead son Eric through the help of mediums. But I realize now her reaching out to Eric this way is a sincerely held belief and a great consolation to her. I also think beliefs like this are far more widespread today than a lot of us know and just there under the surface. And I think of a period in Canadian history, just after World War I, when belief in spiritualism was open and accepted as tens of thousands of grieving parents tried to reach out to sons lost on the Western Front. So, what Joy believes in is not that unusual or unprecedented.

I am also keenly aware and humbled by the words Shakespeare puts in the mouth of Hamlet: *"There are more things in heaven and earth, Horatio/Than are dreamt of in your philosophy."*

What I can tell you is what you will find on these pages is fine, luminous writing coming from the depths of Joy's soul.

There's a great cathartic moment in the book that will live with me for the rest of my life. It's the passage where she returns to the Kenaston Cemetery—the place where members of my own family are buried—just days after her son's death. On that hot August afternoon, she collapses on her son's grave, digs her fingers into the warm dark soil, turns over on her back and, under the great blue dome of the Prairie sky, cries out, "Where are you, my Eric?"

I think anyone, especially anyone born and raised on the Prairies, can't help but be awed by that primal howl, by that screaming sense of aloneness in such an awesome landscape, while at the same time remaining connected and holding on for dear life to what she, the farmer's daughter, knew best—the good earth of Saskatchewan.

I've come to know Joy Pavelich after re-connecting with her more than a year ago and I admire her greatly. She wrote through her pain and thereby helped us understand the lives of people like her and, perhaps, if we happen to be so unfortunate, ourselves. Consequently, I would say having *Chasing My Son Across Heaven* and Joy Pavelich in our world makes it a better place.

—Sean Prpick, Regina,
Treaty 4 Territory, December 2016

Introduction

"When you have eliminated the impossible, whatever
remains, however improbable, must be the truth."
—Sir Arthur Conan Doyle

As a young woman, I studied journalism. That helped
shape a simple belief in me that there are always answers
to be found despite the complexity of any given situation, if you look deep enough.

As years passed, I stuck to that idea and used it as a
tool to continuously search and understand the world
around me. When I decided years later to pursue an
M.A. in communications, not even the fraught nature
of my chosen research topic—the impact of trauma and
how it changed the life experience of those affected by
it—shook this core belief.

Why was I drawn to this area of study?

For me, it was an intersection between the professional and the personal. Previously, I'd watched helplessly as my middle son Eric struggled with a serious,
often debilitating mental illness.

If there was cause and effect here, maybe, I thought, my own research could help lead him to a place of wellness.

Since it was a communications degree, and not psychology, I couldn't ask the questions about "Why?" Instead, I focused my research on processes that might be pathways out of trauma.

I landed on the concept of narrative completion—the telling of stories, and how this helped trauma victims rebuild their fractured identity and, correspondingly, their lives.

When a traumatic event occurs, there is a predictable series of stages. The unusual stress, coupled with the unknown, can overwhelm the individual's ability to cope with or integrate the ideas and emotions involved with that experience. The victim often struggles to find meaning in the event, challenging all their long-held beliefs and assumptions, which, in effect, shatters their identity.

Complicating this, traumatic memories are stored in such a way that the individual faces significant ongoing problems, which are often manifested in extreme mental health problems and/or addiction. The journey out of trauma is complex and can take years to complete.

In cases as severe as this, a powerful healing tool *is* narrative completion—storytelling—which allows the trauma victim to share their experiences in their own words, a process through which sense-making emerges.

As I deepened my academic research, I started to examine the words and writings of three Canadian hockey players who, notoriously, were sexually assaulted by their junior hockey coach, Graham James, during his years working in Western Canada, SK.

These former players were Sheldon Kennedy, Theoren Fleury and Greg Gilhooly.

What I found was evidence that all three did indeed rebuild through the sense-making process of narrative completion. Like others before them, they literally rewrote their life stories. Kennedy, Fleury and Gilhooly moved past the damaging effects of trauma and used their experience as a springboard to become heroes and advocates. A new identity emerged for them, born of reconfiguring the broken pieces of their souls.

What I never expected, though, was that within weeks of my research being done, which completed the requirements for my M.A., I would end up walking the same path as the men I'd studied.

In the early morning hours of August 4, 2013, my middle son, Eric Iain Schmit, took his own life in a lonely corner of rural Saskatchewan.

From that moment on, the world I once believed in was changed, utterly.

Someone once described trauma to me as a one-way doorway. You walk through, but you can never go back. That is so true.

In the immediacy of Eric's death, like each of the men from my research, I was thrown into my own personal chaos. The beliefs I once held of an inherently good and kind world were shattered. I lost the ability to find any sort of meaning in life itself; all the pieces that I had once held dear left with him when he exited this earth.

As I embarked on my own path through trauma and its aftermath, I was intensely aware of the stages I had once researched now becoming the reality of my day-to-day existence: the way things once were, the separation into before and after, my own fractured self as I battled with the same demons of depression, anxiety, and hopelessness that had plagued Eric, and finally the piecing together again of this fractured self into a whole new identity.

The quest for answers which had guided my professional career—both as storyteller and researcher—became a lifeline in my desperate search for a way out of this darkness I'd been thrown into.

What follows is the story of my son Eric and his journey through the challenges of a severe and persistent mental illness.

Even more so, though, it is my story; the chronology of coming to terms, emotionally, spiritually and intellectually, with a loss seemingly too big to bear.

What it isn't is anyone else's story. I've tried not to not speak to anyone else's experience, unless it was part of another bigger story.

This is my sense-making, my own narrative.

1

The Loss

"Sometimes there is no winner in a battle. Sometimes there is just no give from you or your opponent—and then comes a time where you put your swords down and shake hands, acknowledging that you fought with everything you had."

—Eric Schmit

Memory is interesting in how it captures and stores the events of our lives.

August 4, 2013, the day my life separated into the "before" and "after," is one where many details are imbedded vividly in my memory.

The giant chasm was created in the brief moment when I learned that my middle son Eric had ended his life.

I can picture in my mind the calm morning I spent on the deck of our suburban home, sitting quietly in the early sunlight and marveling at the intricate beauty of the spider web on the chain link fence out back as it reflected the light in the dawn's rays.

I recall in intimate detail holding the rosary my youngest son Conner had brought back for me from the Vatican just months before, the ornate silver filigree over the black onyx beads.

I stood up from my chair to go back inside, coffee still in hand, and the rosary fell in pieces at my feet.

I was standing in the landing of the house trying to put the rosary back together as the dogs ran barking to the front door, and I recall my confusion at seeing my cousin Ray there. He was supposed to be at the bedside of his wife Val in the final days of her cancer struggle. The question ran through my head as I went to answer the door: had she passed?

There is an imbedded image of me opening the door, dogs barking at my feet, and him telling me he didn't know what was wrong but that I needed to call my mother, that her and Conner couldn't reach me and were crying.

I looked at him and said, "Eric's dead."

I picked up the phone to dial my mother's home. Mere seconds later, I collapsed on the floor at Ray's feet, laying where the tile from the kitchen separated the oak hardwood in the living room. An indescribable sorrow consumed me in those moments as I lay crumpled, over-whelmed with this awful reality.

I went downstairs to his room, with my cousin beside me, to find some clothes to pack, obsessed with finding black socks to go with his suit and coral-coloured shirt I grabbed from the closet, knowing that this would be the final outfit my handsome son would ever wear. In this drawer, full of socks and underwear, I couldn't find his black dress socks, and Ray gently told me to get myself packed, promising that he would find the socks.

I sent a desperate text message to a long-time pilot friend, Robin Murray, whom I was writing a magazine piece on, to ask if he could fly me to Saskatchewan, where my family lived . . . and where Eric died.

I remember arriving at the farm just a few miles out of town and seeing Robin's brother fuel the airplane, a small four-seat Cessna 180, and the look of incomprehension on all the faces of those in the farm yard, watching in silence.

The flight took slightly over two hours between Strathmore, AB, where we now lived, and Davidson, SK, where family was waiting to meet us.

I cried uncontrollably, resting my head on Robin's chest throughout the flight. It seemed I couldn't find the strength to raise it and sit upright. He kept one arm tight around me, except for the moments when he had to take complete control of the airplane, or when I was exchanging frantic text messages with family and arranging for a close friend of the boys to be there for the oldest, Justin, when we finally could reach him.

The image of Conner's broken tear-stained face when we landed will forever haunt me—him standing with his cousin Josh beside the truck at the edge of the little runway across the road from the farm my ex-husband had grown up on, and 20 miles away from where our families were starting to gather at my mother's home.

Can I ever erase the memory of my youngest child running towards the airplane as we pulled to a stop and then, when I opened the door, of us falling into each other's arms?

The priest at my mother's farm, my many relatives already there, and my dear friends Val and Randy—the first I had called—eventually taking me to the hospital back in Davidson so I could be sedated for the night. I'll never forget these people. Nor will I the sweet nurse who asked if she could use Reiki—a Japanese healing technique—as I lay there devastated in that hospital room. And the message I received from Sheldon Kennedy offering to be there for me and my sons Justin and Conner, to which I replied, "Who would have thought I'd live my own research?"

This vivid recall, the entrenched memories—I know from my research that this is how trauma is stored in the brain—fractured images with intense emotions attached. The brain—memory—has its own storage system for life-changing moments such as these.

What I *can't* remember, though, are the words that changed my life forever.

I don't remember being told the words that my son was dead.

Somewhere, within the 24 hours that made up August 4, 2013, are a select few seconds so painful they have been relegated to a place buried deep in my subconscious from where they may never resurface.

That day—that moment in time—created a giant vortex, where questions, guilt, sorrow and blame found their home in the aftermath of the tragic end of Eric's long-standing battle with mental illness.

When Eric's story ended, mine began.

While I had always had a belief in the afterlife and lived a quiet respectful Catholicism, that faith had never been truly tested.

Eric's death changed everything.

Suddenly, personal and professional morphed into a single messy search for answers to the most difficult questions I'd ever faced in my life. The faith which I had once taken for granted was now wide open for interpretation.

Is there something more? Where do you go when you die? Is there a Heaven, or is this all there is?

Where are you, my precious son?

Have you found this safe place we were promised, and you so believed in?

Or are you simply gone, the oft-mentioned soul merely an empty promise from a God I now struggle with my entire being to believe in?

My beautiful son journeyed through a disease of the mind and soul which ended in a life cut short.

It is my heart's desire that telling his story and my own will stimulate compassion, understanding and hope for others who have, or will someday walk this path. In sharing these stories, it too is my hope that those who survive the tragic loss of a loved one will find comfort in my struggle through the aftermath of grief, along with hope and a renewed faith that love indeed never ends.

It is not meant to be an examination of religion, or to contradict the teachings of my Catholic faith, or anyone else's. If one were to examine it through the lens of religion, perhaps it would be best thought of that I followed a path of mystical theology to rebuild a worldview that was consistent with my new reality.

If anything, I would hope this account brings others back to a faith in their own understanding of the world, their lives and the lives of the people around them.

2

The Many Sides of Eric

"The Warrior's Code
You're a fighter.
You've got the Spirit of a warrior;
the champion's heart."
—Eric Schmit

The Warrior

From the moment he entered this world, Eric was destined to be a fighter. It was what earned him the nickname many years later of "The Warrior." He showed no interest in getting here on time; several weeks prior to his birth the doctors had been concerned he may arrive early given his size. That concern, however, proved to be groundless. As we celebrated Thanksgiving weekend at my parents' farm, he was already two weeks past his due date. I was scheduled to meet with the doctor the next morning to arrange for inducement when my water broke in the middle of the night, precipitating a hurried trip to University Hospital in Saskatoon.

It was quickly obvious there was something not quite right, although no one spoke of it to his father and me. The nurses hustled and bustled around, and the doctor was called. They finally shared that the umbilical cord was wrapped around this baby's neck. The heart rate was monitored carefully to determine when action would have to take place. Eventually, slightly blue from a lack of oxygen, he made his way down the birth canal. At 4:35 a.m., October 13, 1992, Eric Iain Schmit entered the world at 9 pounds, 8 ounces.

Although it took a few minutes, when his colour finally came, Eric graced the world as a beautiful, round, pink baby boy. Everyone was ecstatic—no one more so, however, than his big brother Justin, who had been praying for, and waiting for, a baby brother. My cousin Celeste, who had stayed with Justin when we went to the hospital, brought him to see us before he went to school, so he could see this long-awaited answer to his prayers. It was rosary day at Saint Bernard School, the Catholic elementary that Justin attended, and the gift Justin later brought back to the hospital for Eric and I was a small blue plastic rosary. That perfect offering set the stage for a long-standing family tradition of sharing rosaries as gifts of remembrance.

Within 24 hours, we were released from the hospital and sent home. Our first activity was to take Eric to "Show and Tell" with Justin so he could share his prized new brother with the world.

Raising Justin had been an easy job, his disposition given towards pleasing those around him. Eric, on the other hand, was his own person from the beginning. Far from the approximately 16 hours of sleep a baby less than six months of age should require, Eric didn't really sleep at all. And so, with Eric, the first months were exhausting. Our nighttime ritual was him propped up in a baby bouncer, facing me so that his eyes could always be on me. He always needed to have me in his sight or he became distressed. I laid on the couch in the tiny apartment we lived in at the time, watching late night repeats of *Roseanne*, trying to stay awake with him. If my eyes happened to close, his sharp cries awoke me, and I saw his dark piercing eyes staring right back at me, fixated on my face.

Eventually, I turned to holding him in my arms so that I could grab a few minutes of sleep. His physical size made it impossible to nurse him beyond the first six weeks. However, propped up in my arms with a bottle and formula, with the occasional "wolf nap" as we called it, Eric happily ate and I had moments of rest. His inability to sleep definitely made Eric's early years a more challenging period than my first experience with parenting.

His nature was different, too, though. There was a sensitivity about Eric that emerged in infancy and was characteristic throughout his life. It was inexplicable how he would be able to sense and feel the emotions around him, even in his earliest days. I would sometimes sit him in his bouncer beside the piano while I played. I was amazed the first time that I played a song that had a mournful tone. He burst into tears. I changed the song to a more upbeat one. He stopped crying and simply watched me, those penetrating brown eyes fixated on my every move. I played a sad song, and he cried. And on and on it went. At less than six months of age, Eric could sense the emotional tone of music, or perhaps of me, the pianist; the first hint at a connection between us that couldn't be explained or defined.

In later years, I experienced this again. I remember coming home from work, parking in the garage and walking into the house, worried about something that had happened that day. Eric was in the office of our bungalow, and as I walked in, he called out to me, "Are you okay, Mom, what's wrong?" This lifelong connection between Eric and I transcended language.

A Strong-Willed Child

Strong-willed would have been a polite euphemism to describe Eric as a toddler. Tantrums were commonplace, as were incidents of him holding his breath until he turned blue or banging his head on the floor when he wanted his way. But he was equally loving and needed to be close to his family. Somewhere in this timeframe, his father gave him the nickname "Boogs," which we called him throughout his life.

Needless to say, Eric's strong will often meant the rest of the family gave in to his wants merely because the fight was too exhausting. Along with this inflexibility or stubbornness, he was resistant to change of any kind. Simple things such as moving his and his younger brother Conner's bunk beds from top and bottom to side by side were monumental events when dealing with Eric. As a young child, he had his own fork that he ate with, and his own place at the table.

From his earliest days, Eric had a penchant for storytelling. When he was very little, I was getting him and Justin ready to go to the babysitter's so that I go could go to work. He had on this little blue sports jacket and I was buttoning it up as I sat him on the table. He looked at me and said, "I can't go to there anymore, Mom. She hits me."

Justin was frozen in the middle of the kitchen, staring at Eric.

"With a baseball bat," Eric added for increased effect. And then, in his little face, you could see the internal recognition and awareness that he had likely gone too far. "But there's never any blood," he finished with and looked at Justin and I with this look of having completed his story.

We determined that their cousins were coming to visit later that day and Eric didn't want to miss a moment with them. This clever story that grabbed both Justin's and my attention almost bought him the reprieve from the babysitter. This was an early lesson; when Eric had a wild story, there was usually an underlying motive we needed to look deeper to find. For years, when something Eric said seemed a bit too hard to believe, Justin would look at Eric and smile.

"Does this involve a baseball bat?" he would ask.

Eric was two and a half years old when his place as the baby of the family was disrupted by the birth of easy-going, good-natured Conner. This displacement wasn't something he took well. From putting Conner in the dryer and convincing him they were playing hide and seek, while coming to ask me how to turn it on, to the foot out to trip him while Conner was learning to walk, it took Eric a good while to adapt to the newest sibling. But in time, the two became inseparable. Or rather, the three became inseparable. As Justin and Conner remarked in Eric's eulogy, they were never referred to as "Justin, Eric or Conner," but rather as "the three Schmit boys." The brotherhood was formed early on and the brotherly bond remained strong through a myriad of life experiences.

Although this period of our lives was hallmarked by several moves between Eastern and Western Canada and Australia for their father Doug's work, these early years were some of the best of all of our lives. These early glimpses into the things that made Eric "Eric" were also the pieces that coloured our lives. While he may have had personality quirks that made him challenging, his creativity and imagination were unsurpassed and that brought all our lives so much energy and joy.

The Superhero

For the vast majority of his early years, he lived with a superhero alter ego. He learned to spell by leaving little notes around the house, written on the doors, his tiny printing stating, "Eric is Batman." He would often get me to script his superhero stories in tiny books he would build out of yellow sticky notes stapled together, filled with his artwork, while he directed me to "write" as he dictated stories of heroism. He lived by day in a bat suit, sewn by his grandmother and supplemented by costume pieces purchased at Halloween and Christmas. For a few years, Eric really was Batman!

At his funeral, his brother Justin shared the story of how, as little boys, Eric and Conner were at one of his hockey games. As Conner played quietly in the stands, Eric ran up and down the rows of bleachers with a small plastic Batman in his hand, oblivious to the world around him, his bat suit on and his cape flowing behind him. A group of women watched the boys, and then asked Conner what he was going to be for Halloween.

Eric spun around, hands on his hips, cape snapping around his legs. "Aren't you going to ask what I'm going to be?" he asked.

"Batman," the women all replied in unison.

"No, you dress up for Halloween," he said. "I *am* Batman. I'm going to be a knight in shining armour." And off he flew down the stands to return to his superhero exploits. Throughout his early life, he could enter this created imaginary world at will.

Eric was born late in the year, which meant he was eligible to start kindergarten at four years old. I was concerned about him starting school this early, especially given that he had an incredible attachment to me, and so kept a close eye on how he did in class. I was ready to make the decision to keep him home an extra year if need be. Intellectually, Eric was more than ready. However, as expected, he did struggle with being apart from me. His kindergarten year proved to be trying, in that he often had phantom illnesses early in the morning on school days. As Eric was extremely adept at presenting as ill, I had trouble deciphering whether the illnesses were real or conjured up as a reason to stay home.

One morning, we had a difficult time outside of the school. Eric wanted to come home, pleading sick, and I insisted he go to class. Around 11 a.m., I received a call from the school. I was being called to pick him up. It wasn't because Eric was sick, though. It was because he was being disciplined.

Apparently, as Eric made his way into the classroom, somewhat teary-eyed, the teacher asked him what was wrong.

"I wanted to stay home today and Mom made me come to school," he sobbed.

"Well, I think your mom was probably right," his teacher gently told him, at which point Eric collapsed, inconsolably wailing, "Our house has burned down and nobody cares."

The boys' school, St. Stephen's, was a small Catholic school. While Eric was in kindergarten and Justin in Grade 7, they were in the same building. The teacher immediately sent for Justin.

"How is everyone?" she asked.

"Fine," Justin replied cautiously, not certain where the conversation was going.

"Where are you staying?"

Another confusing question, to which Justin replied, "At home."

"Oh, then the fire wasn't too bad?" she asked.

The next step was a call to mom, who brought Eric home from his first visit to the principal's office. As I sat there with the adults and Eric, I was amazed that he had managed to spin this tale so convincingly. However, having been on the receiving end of his tall tales before, I knew that being drawn into the story was easily done.

The Cowboy

That winter, we decided to make a permanent move back to Western Canada. Our new home was about an hour outside of Calgary, in a place called Strathmore, a bedroom community filled with workers (like us) from the big city. The timing of the move, however, meant that we couldn't move into our new home until late August, just in time for the boys' school year. The balance of the summer was spent with both families in Saskatchewan.

Small town rodeos are part of the rural culture of the West. The boys had been watching the movie *8 Seconds*, the story of Lane Frost. Frost was one of the world's best bull riders, who, at 25 years of age, was killed in Cheyenne, Wyoming. Frost was known for his trademark dismount, where he would face the crowd with both arms in the air and wave to them. On his final ride, as he dismounted the Brahma bull, it turned and hit him in the side with a horn, breaking several of his ribs, which in turn punctured his heart and lungs. Frost's death in the rodeo arena, and the story of it, was the stuff of legends and so he became one to Eric.

As we waited to move to our new home, the boys were making most of their summer, living it up, enjoying rural Saskatchewan. My father was a cowboy, so we made a plan to treat him to the rodeo in Watrous, a small community about a half hour from my parents' home. At this point in his life, Eric had moved past the Batman stage and now was fully immersed in his alter ego as a cowboy, based on the Lane Frost persona. Eric was planning on sheep riding—the children's version of bull riding at these events.

Sheep riding was one of the highlight events of any rodeo, often held between the bronc riding and the bull busting. The announcer spoke to each of the competitors in turn. As he got to Eric, he asked him several questions. In answering, Eric indicated he was an old hand at this. In some aspects he was, as rodeos were often basement events with the brothers wrestling, or Grandma Carmella's retriever sent out after a bottle or a ball with a small boy on his back. As for sheep riding, he had never actually participated in a real event.

The rest of the competitors took a typical position: they lay on top of the sheep, their legs wrapped around its belly and arms wrapped around the sheep's neck. The result of this would be a small child falling slowly to one side or the other as the sheep raced across the arena. Eric, following the lead of his new Lane Frost persona, instead assumed the position he had seen so often on TV. He had his little gloves wrapped upside down underneath the rope, which was wound across the sheep's belly. He sat upright, hat on straight, and when he was ready, he nodded to the rodeo hands.

"Okay, boys," he calmly said, the Lane Frost phrase meaning to let the animal loose.

Eric successfully made it across to the end of the arena, the only rider to do so. As he dismounted, he turned and faced the crowd, assumed the Lane Frost position and waved to the fans in the bleachers. He brought the crowd to their knees. Even the rodeo clown was laughing so hard he had tears streaming down his face, down on one knee with his head in his hands.

The Story Teller and Actor

Sports were just a part of the Schmit boys' lives. If it wasn't track and field, it was baseball, or rodeo. Of all the sports they participated in, though, it really was hockey that was the mainstay in our household. All three of the boys spent a great deal of their lives in arenas spanning across Canada. We chose Strathmore as our home as much because of the twin arena complex as for any other reason. The boys were on hockey teams that often held the same group of players year after year. This meant that while the players formed friendships, so too did the families.

When Eric was about nine years old, one of the moms came and asked how I was doing. I wasn't sure what was up. Apparently, Eric had convinced his entire hockey team, and coaches, that he had been diagnosed with cancer. However, he had cautioned them all, "Please don't talk to my mom about it as it upsets her so badly." The secret lived for several weeks, with many locker room updates as to his ongoing health care, until one of my dear friends decided she had to check in out of concern for me.

Eric's creative ability, the act of throwing himself completely into a character or a story, wasn't something he left with him in childhood. As he entered junior high, he showed a natural affinity for drama and theatre at school. So much so that his principal called and suggested I send him to a drama camp in Calgary for the summer. He had just given Eric 100 percent in drama. He received the school award, and the principal told me he saw Eric as a prodigy, something he had never labeled a student before. As I watched the final talent show at the drama camp, I reveled in his ability to own the stage, something that was so hard for me to fathom as an introvert. And, as Eric was natured much like me, with that natural draw towards introspection and aloofness, it was remarkable to watch him leave it behind as he took the stage. As we drove home together that night, I asked him how he did it, how he could assume a personality or engage in a story so convincingly.

"I just imagine that it's real, Mom, and then it is," he replied.

Whatever it was that Eric put his mind to, there were no half measures. This intensity was known to flare during times of stress. Hockey tryouts were particularly difficult for Eric to navigate. But we saw it at other times too, like when Justin had to leave for boarding school after a visit home, or went to pursue his own hockey dreams. We were starting to see Eric's intensity manifest now in extreme anxiety, from nausea, to other digestive disorders, to an inability to sleep.

In hindsight, much of the behaviour we saw in Eric is typically present in people who develop mental health disorders later in life—the sensitivity, the creativity, the intensity. At the time, in our relative innocence, however, we embraced the uniqueness and character of Eric, his idiosyncrasies that made him funny, charming and irrepressibly sweet. He was a complex but brilliant child, and later young man, who lived life full speed ahead, who loved with his entire being, who brought magic and beauty to all the lives he touched, and who truly coloured outside of the lines in everything he did.

In the earliest days of grief, these memories of the precocious Eric were the hardest to face, the times when he had brought light and laughter to our lives. As the days slowly turned to months and years, the same memories took the edge off the sharpness of the pain and became once again a source of small pieces of joy.

3

Darkness Comes

"The thing I hate the most is anxiety, there's always something that triggers it. I'm not sure why, but it suddenly becomes a panic. It is hard to get rid of, and it's like having absolutely no control over anything. It's a fear of dying. Funny how I go from one side of the spectrum to the other. From being suicidal to being afraid to die."

—Eric Schmit

His Own Perfect Storm

The onset of symptoms with Eric was rapid. Although there was a quirkiness to his personality, it was what made him such a lovely little boy. We didn't think to question it. Why would we?

In a family of boys dominated by the love of hockey, there was a single National Hockey League team that held the heart of all the boys, especially Eric. He was an avid fan of the Montreal Canadiens, and so for his 13th birthday, he and I flew to Ottawa when the Habs—short for le Habitants, the Francophone version of the team name—were playing the Senators so he could see them in a live game. The ticket agent who sold me the tickets knew it was a birthday gift, and even ensured we would be seated amongst Montreal fans for the game.

As an added bonus, Saku Koivu was back in the lineup after his lengthy fight with cancer. It was the gift to top all gifts for Eric, to watch his beloved Canadiens and see Koivu play. Koivu had earned a spot in everyone's hearts when he had taken the time to send Eric and Conner a personal thank you note for the packages of pictures they had drawn and sent him as a get-well gesture.

The night was fun and perfect. The next morning, we awoke early, and Eric and I drove along the St. Lawrence Seaway to Sainte-Anne-de-Beaupré, a site east of Quebec City where a church was erected in honour of St. Anne, Mary's mother and grandmother of Jesus.

A beautiful history came with the church. The site was chosen in the 1600s when a group of sailors were lost at sea on the St. Lawrence and prayed to St. Anne for a miracle, promising that they would build a shrine in her honour, should she spare their lives. True to their word, following their deliverance, the sailors built a church, which has drawn pilgrims from around the world to witness many miracles in the sacred place.

Eric had a special connection to his faith. We spent hours in the old church, where relics that represented miraculous healings hung from the pillars, and then walked the grounds as Eric kept my camera his constant companion, capturing photo after photo of this sacred place. As Justin would say, God was the only thing Eric didn't question.

It was a weekend we cherished, every piece of it touching something precious to Eric.

We returned home and life was to go back to normal. I dropped him off at school and headed to work, which was just a few minutes away. I couldn't believe it when the principal called; Eric was absent. I couldn't fathom this. I had watched him leave and to this day can still picture the little blonde head, his brown Columbia ski jacket and his armful of books. How could a child literally disappear between the vehicle and the front door of the school?

This was completely out of character for Eric, and so everyone's alarm bells were going off. Eric saw the world in black and white, and following the rules was important to him. The principal broke into his locker to see if we could find any clue as to where he had gone. I was absolutely terrified, driving madly through town, from work, to home, to school, back home and all the spaces in between, desperately hoping for a glimpse or a sign of him. Finally, we phoned the local RCMP detachment and a member was sent out. Several hours later, Eric reappeared. He had been hiding in the church a block away from the school. Later, we learned that Eric had a strong fight-or-flight response, and when the world became overwhelming, he would act on that urge to run.

Although there may have been signs before that we didn't see, that day it was undeniable. Something had changed. It was as though a switch had been turned off. The gentle, pensive Eric was now obviously gloomy. He was moody and had bouts of anger. He retreated into a shell. He began to avoid school, and his once treasured friendships became a source of angst for him.

There were times when he was the subject of school bullying, typical for that age group. As much as I wanted to intervene, Eric begged me not to, fearing the behaviour would be even worse. Then, one day, there was an incident of name-calling and Eric ran all the way home from school. Conner was heartsick and scared, riding the bus without his brother, and as soon as he got into the house he found him locked in the bathroom, where Eric was crying his eyes out.

That was the tipping point for me and I immediately phoned the principal, a remarkable man who had a soft spot for Eric and who went to great lengths to make sure Eric was always safe and felt welcomed at school. The following morning, within minutes of the boys who had caused Eric so much grief arriving in school, they were on the receiving end of a significant dressing down. After that, they simply ignored him. I'm not sure which was worse, the shaming or the acting as though he didn't exist.

The Undeniable Unknown

November 2006, at just 14 years of age, Eric made his first suicide attempt. He drank a bottle of cold medicine and went back to school, where he passed out on the bathroom floor, vomiting. I don't remember whether it was a student or staff that found him, but while waiting for me to arrive, he shared with the principal that this had been an attempt to take his life.

This disclosure was taken seriously, and he went to the Foothills Hospital Emergency Department in Calgary. A friend who worked as a nurse knew of the Young Adolescent Program there for youth with mental health issues and had suggested he be taken there. However, after a long assessment, Eric was not admitted into the program, and instead given a prescription for Celexa, a new generation antidepressant, and was sent home.

Rather than have a calming effect, however, what we experienced was an increased instability in Eric's moods. They now swung from low to very low to outbursts of anger, which seemed like his childhood tantrums upped a notch. Electronics took a beating and had a short life cycle with Eric, phones being commonly smashed in a fit of anger. He once kicked out the car windshield as I tried to get him to help. The doctors called him a "rapid cycler," with these swings happening quickly and unpredictably.

A little more than a month later, on December 22, the depression was so severe his father, Conner and I took him to the Children's Hospital in Calgary. Again, following a long wait, and a discussion with the doctor where I shared my concerns about the Celexa, the doctor argued that the medicine was correct, but the dosage was too low. Eric's dose was doubled.

Christmas was near and his older brother and mentor would be flying home from the southern United States, where he was playing hockey. Eric didn't want to stay in the hospital, nor did we want him there. While we managed to keep him home through Christmas, the next three weeks became increasingly difficult as we struggled to understand what was going on. By mid-January, it was back to the emergency department at the Foothills Hospital. This time, Eric was admitted.

The widely recognized Children's Global Assessment Scale rates a child's mental state. By this time, Eric's rating was abysmally low, 15 out of 100. Although there was a waiting list at the time of approximately 300 young people, the severity of Eric's depression was enough that he was catapulted to the top of the list and took residence in one of the 15 available beds for youths with mental health challenges.

The next several months could only be described as a nightmare our family couldn't wake up from, as we navigated not only through the medical challenges of mental illness, but also through a Children's Services investigation. The stresses on the family precipitated the unraveling of my marriage to my partner Doug. Already not a frequent presence in the boys' lives up until this point, when the marriage ended so too did his connection to the children. Eric shared with me that while most children pray for their families to stay together, he had spent his childhood praying that I would leave his father. *Fait accompli*, our family now just consisted of "Joy and the boys," as we were referred to by both family and friends.

Eric was in and out of the hospital for several months as his medical team and I worked hand-in-hand, trying desperately to find the answers to the riddle of his emotional and mental state. It was at the hospital that his second suicide attempt occurred—in the bathroom of his room where he hanged himself in the shower. Although the children weren't allowed to enter each other's rooms and certainly never a bathroom, for reasons we will never know, another child named Max made that unusual choice that evening and found Eric unconscious. The boy, who had been hospitalized with Selective Mutism, had not spoken in years, yet, without words, he alerted the nursing staff.

When I arrived at the hospital and sat at Eric's side, he told me, "Mom, someday when I'm out of here, I'm going to write a song and call it 'Max's Song'. It's going to be music without words."

Other than the grief journey after he passed, the pain of watching Eric struggle in these earliest days of his illness was one of the most horrific periods in my life. I felt absolute helplessness as a mother, wanting so desperately to make it better for him but at a complete loss as to how to do that.

As a family, Justin, Conner and I wrapped ourselves around Eric. Conner and I drove the hour to Calgary every night after I was done work to visit with him, and if things were going well we would bring Eric home for the weekends. Although Justin was playing hockey in the United States, he spoke to Eric every night on the hospital phone, offering encouragement and unconditional love. When Eric had made the near suicide attempt in the bathroom, Justin flew home to be with him. His brothers and I had the awful experience of watching him in "high observations," an area of the unit where there were three rooms with glass walls so that the children could be observed at all times by the nursing staff, sleeping on mattresses on the floor—the only items in the rooms. Eric watching us leave from behind the glass, long blonde hair in disarray, clothed in a blue hospital gown, was soul-destroying. And yet, we had no other options. We were just trying to keep him alive.

Another Attempt

By the spring of that year, I realized it was impossible for me to stay in a job. Managing Eric's mental health needs and trying to maintain a sense of stability for the other two was all I had in me to do; I had to let something go. I left the position I had as an editor at a safety training centre, not knowing when I would be able to return, so that I could give my full attention to our struggling family. This decision to stay home probably saved Eric's life one more time. I had left my job on the Friday, and immediately started working with his school and the medical team on a plan to integrate him back home and into school.

The following week, he wasn't doing well. I was on the phone in my home office, trying to call the number I had been provided by the psychiatric team at the hospital for support when he was in crisis. However, I quickly discovered that the service they advised me to access didn't apply to outlying areas like our rural home. After several minutes of trying to decipher what help was available, and realizing there was none, I stood up in frustration and hung up the phone.

As I walked back towards the kitchen where Eric was, for some reason I thought to look in my purse, which was laying on the floor near the entry landing. Everything was kept locked in the safe, but his daily medications were in a compartment of my purse. The zipper was open and I saw that both bottles of Eric's medications were empty.

I immediately ran into the kitchen, where I found he had cut himself, and was calmly sitting at the table with a completed suicide note in hand. With two empty bottles of pills in my hands, and a son covered in blood, I called 911. The area we had moved into was under construction, and our home was one of the first finished. It still didn't have a house number on it. There were two construction workers building a house across the street that I flagged down. They ran over and sat inside with my son while I waited for the ambulance to arrive. I'm not sure why I didn't direct them to wait for the ambulance and why I didn't sit with Eric. Perhaps I simply couldn't cope. From the time they were little and getting needles or giving blood, to bigger and fighting or playing hockey, it has always been nearly impossible for me to be present when they were experiencing pain.

I will always be eternally grateful for those two men and the compassion and care they shared with Eric and I that morning. I've often wondered how many times they might reflect on that day and wonder how the story turned out.

The ambulance and police took him to the hospital and a close family friend came with me. Eric was given charcoal orally to absorb the medication he had ingested and lay in a drug-induced sleep. As I sat there holding his hand and watching him sleep, blood tests were run to see if he was taking illicit drugs, as everything was up for question at this time, his behaviour so inexplicable. Everything came back clear, underscoring that this was not an outward but inward battle Eric was fighting, his own brain chemistry his opponent.

After several hours, he was stable enough to be sent to Calgary and once again hospitalized in the youth program. Eric's mental illness was proving itself to be persistent and resistant to treatment.

This journey into the world of mental illness was such foreign territory. And I felt so lost as I tried to understand and navigate. I think the most common question I asked was, "Why?" What made my son develop this mental illness? What was the cause?

The Fight of His Life

For two years, Eric had periods of wellness and periods of deep lows. When he was well, he was funny, articulate, deeply intelligent and thoughtful. He drew people to him like a light. When he wasn't well, he plunged into an abyss, excessively sad, sleeping all the time, obsessed with illness and death, and experiencing episodes of rage. The rage was never directed at us as individuals, but the doors and walls in our house took a beating. He seemed to need somewhere to direct this frustration and anger. I now know anger is common with bipolar disorder, the most likely diagnosis. Eric's highs were higher than the rest of us experienced and he carried us along with the passion and exuberance he had for life when he was like this. His lows plummeted us all into helplessness and fear as we tried desperately to reach him in this darkness.

From the time they were small boys, Justin had always assumed a mentor role with both of his brothers, and especially so with Eric. Their father's absence meant that, as much a brother, Justin was the one who gave Eric the guidance one would normally expect from a father, doling out his own teenaged views on sports, girls and life. He took care of his brothers for me so that I could get things done or travel for work. At his young age, he filled the role of second parent as well as sibling, a complex combination. I relied heavily on Justin for that extra support.

The summer before his Grade 12 year, Eric went to stay with Justin, who had retired from hockey and was now living and working in Mexico. His medical needs were intense, and I needed some respite. It was only when Eric was with Justin that I felt I could let my own guard down and rest. Justin had married the summer before, and his wife Miranda, their little boy Owen and her family were all there. I knew Justin was as deeply invested in Eric's well-being as I was, and Miranda and her family too were all genuinely loving, caring and supportive.

Conner and I went to join them in Mexico for the last two weeks of summer while I did a photo shoot for a Canadian drilling company's Mexican operations. While there it was obvious: the old Eric was back! The switch which had gone off a few years earlier was without a doubt now back on. He seemed happy again. There was laughter and sharing, and the somber, morose Eric that had replaced our shining light seemed to have gone away.

Grade 12 was a comeback year for Eric. Naturally talented on the ice, he had started young and generally played on the highest-level teams throughout his minor hockey days. The mental health challenges sidelined that to a certain extent. However, his love of hockey gave him purpose, and regardless of what was going on personally, he managed to play in some capacity throughout the troubled years. As a result, he managed to make the A-level when he went back and played his final year of midget hockey on the local team.

Somehow, despite the multiple hospital admissions and the deep-seated depression through the two to three years of upheaval, he also managed to graduate with his original class—with the necessary credits to attend university if he so desired. This offered insight into Eric's intellectual capacity and intelligence.

However, in that moment, education wasn't on Eric's radar. With his lifelong passion for hockey, and with a brother who had made a career playing professionally, he wanted to follow in his footsteps. The year following his graduation, he wanted to take time off school and pursue his love of hockey. Of course, we supported that decision; he had been through so much, had sacrificed so much, we all wanted him to experience the happiness that had eluded him during those important teenage years.

Consistent with their relative youth, Justin and Miranda's marriage was tumultuous, and short-lived. It ended around the time of Eric's graduation, and weeks after their second child, daughter Mia, was born. Miranda left shortly afterward with the two children to live in Newfoundland, where her entire family was.

Despite the distance, Eric maintained a close relationship with Miranda and the kids.

Ah, That Trip!

One weekend in late September, Justin, Eric and Conner loaded up my tiny Volkswagen Jetta diesel—three big men and a tiny car filled with suitcases and hockey equipment as they headed to Helena, Montana. Eric had a tryout with a team one of Justin's former teammates was now coaching. The boys all said they had the time of their lives that weekend. Justin said if he ever had a bad day, all he ever had to do was think about the three days they spent together, some of the best of his life. They came back with an arsenal of stories from the days they spent together.

Eric had the driest sense of humour of all. They loved to tell the story of how, during the trip, they were having lunch in a Subway and a man with long dark hair, a beard and sandals came in.

"Look, guys, it's our Lord and Saviour Jesus Christ," Eric whispered to his brothers. When the restaurant worker at the till asked the bearded man what he wanted, Eric said to his brothers, his voice ringing out, in what happened to be a moment of absolute quiet in the restaurant, "A loaf of bread and a bottle of wine."

In lieu of a spot on the team, the coach recommended Eric go to a team in Bremerton, Washington in the NORPAC League to improve his skill level. Eric wasn't disappointed, and the adventure moved on to Phase Two. He just wanted a place to play the game he loved. The three boys made the long drive back to Canada and I immediately made arrangements for him to fly out of Calgary into Seattle to start this chapter in his eighteenth year.

From the moment he arrived, Eric loved the game, his teammates and his coaches. He even wore the Captain's "C". Most importantly, he found a home with the family of his teammate Ethan, on their farm south of Tacoma, Washington. It was a perfect fit, with Eric and Ethan being the team tough guys and best friends.

Although Eric had just left for Seattle, his birthday was within days of his departure. And it also fell on the Canadian Thanksgiving long weekend. Conner and I decided to take a 15-hour drive to watch a few of his games and help him celebrate his 18th birthday. It was dark as we made our way around the horseshoe between Seattle and Tacoma and eventually up to Bremerton where the team's home rink was located. As we walked through the arena doors, we arrived just in time for Conner to witness Eric's first goal of the season, and first of the weekend. He was on fire, having us there to watch him.

After the game, we found a hotel room, and over the course of the long weekend managed to celebrate his birthday by doing some shopping, enjoying a dinner with his billet brother Ethan and his mom, going to the movies, getting in one more of Eric's home games, purchasing him a new phone and simply regaling in each other's company.

Monday morning arrived and it was time for Conner and I to head home. We all drove to the farm where Eric was staying. It was lush and green, with a light fog hanging over the quaint country landscape. Eric and Ethan bid us farewell from the middle of the driveway. It was hard to leave, but he was happy where he was.

The Obvious Trigger

The three boys were exceedingly close to each other, and all exceedingly close to me. We spoke every day, often more than once, and texted each other throughout the day. Usually there was a call at night so we knew everyone was okay. Whenever Justin and Eric were playing hockey, they always called to let me know that they were safe and well. There was never a conversation that didn't end with an "I love you."

This closeness was often remarked on by people. Rarely had they seen such closeness in a family, and especially amongst siblings. That deep love, however, is also the source of profound pain in the grieving process; cavernous grief is evidence of what once was a great bond.

When Eric came home for Christmas, we were excited to have him back, even for a few days. It was reminiscent of the times Justin was away playing hockey and when he would return we had those few glorious days again as a family—I felt complete in the times when my three boys and I were together.

Although Eric was only home for a few days, I did notice the heavy drinking. I was concerned, but I told myself that it was just because he had a few days at home and was catching up with his friends. When the season ended a few months later, and he returned home for the summer, it was obvious the drinking was a problem. But with teenage boys in rural Alberta, it's also a rite of passage. If he was focused on a goal, he wouldn't drink, but when he did drink, he would hit it hard. And what would set him onto drinking was unpredictable.

Although a doctor had once told me that if you see mental illness, think addiction, and if you see addiction, think mental health, I didn't connect the two in Eric's behaviour. I don't think I really understood how intricately the two were entwined—mental illness and substance misuse. Instead, I focused on his drinking as the reason for the erratic behaviour, as that was when it emerged.

Outside of the drinking, Eric and I rarely fought. He was always calm and thoughtful and reasonable. But we came to anticipate when Eric was going to take that first drink, and usually, we knew the outcome wasn't going to be good. It had such a strange effect on his brain circuitry. It made him unpredictable and impulsive.

One night, he noisily came into the house, obviously having been drinking, and Eric and I started arguing. Conner woke up and the argument got worse. I got scared and phoned 911. Eric grabbed the phone and ran outside, calling Justin for guidance as the police arrived. As they went around the side of the house, Eric dropped the phone. Justin could hear the fight ensue as Eric grabbed each of the RCMP constables by their shirts and held them up off the ground. One of them took a club and hit Eric across the forehead, knocking him to the ground and leaving a massive gash. They took him to the police station to stay overnight in the drunk tank. He was charged with assaulting a peace officer. The next morning, I not only had to go to work, but I also knew me picking Eric up would have been disastrous. I begged the police not to release him until Justin could get there, as I was worried that the incident might make him suicidal in its aftermath.

To understand Eric, you would have to understand that even his demons were angelic, for lack of a better description. When he emerged from the chaos, he was always the Eric we loved so desperately—sweet, remorseful, as confused by his own behaviour as we were. Being charged criminally meant huge problems if he wanted to continue to play hockey, and I didn't want to be the reason my son had to live the rest of his life with a criminal record. I found a lawyer in town, John Getz, whom I engaged to work with Eric. Like the rest of us, John took to him, seeing him outside the madness of his illness, and at his best.

The one hope I had was that perhaps now, with a judge reviewing his case, he would be sent for care by the courts. The judge, it seemed, couldn't help but be enamoured with Eric. Standing there, facing the judge, dressed in his suit with his hair immaculate, holding his grandmother's rosary in his hand, Eric was as remorseful as possible as we listened to the charges being read.

There was this moment when describing the incident outside our house that caused the courtroom to erupt in laughter. One of the officer's notes reflected that after they hit Eric with the club, Eric simply looked at them and said, "Hit me again, you pussy. I've been hit harder by girls."

Instead of the help I had hoped for, the judge gently spoke to Eric about how his brain seemed to have an allergy to alcohol, and that he would have to figure out that it didn't make him a better person. The judge went on to say how he wished he could take Eric travelling and show him the world that was available to him out there, pointing to me, his mother, and the love and support that was there for him. The charge was reduced by the judge and Eric paid a significant fine, but that was the end of the incident.

Although there were other episodes, I think this one really brings to mind some of the bigger picture issues with mental illness—primarily the criminalization of it and how that unnecessarily ties up our judicial processes when this is a medical issue. It penalizes the mentally ill for being sick. And it also underscores that our prime resource is the police, but they often are not trained to deal with individuals in mental health crisis, and are doing their part of serve and protect despite the complexities they face when responding.

Alcohol obviously made the mental health journey more difficult, and I couldn't grasp why Eric simply wouldn't choose to not drink, when the outcomes were always so worrisome. What I didn't know at the time was that the alcohol wasn't the problem in itself. Eric's behaviour was text book as a coping strategy for his mental illness: self-medicating.

Physically Strong

Despite the occasional alcohol-induced flare-ups, Eric seemed to have put a significant distance between himself and his early teenage struggles. One way he did so was to immerse himself in his physical pursuits. He was training for hockey, training for fighting, and working out in either our local gym or at MMAU—Mixed Martial Arts University—in Calgary where he and Justin, working again in the Alberta oil patch, trained. Deeply spiritual, Eric also found many different yoga practices beneficial, whether the intensity of Bikram, or the calming of Yin.

After a year out of school, and various labour-type jobs, he decided he was ready to pursue a post-secondary education. He had always been creative and artistic, as well as physical. And he loved the English language. He kept elaborate journals and wrote poetically and fluidly. He had just completed a personal training certification program and was thrilled when he was accepted to take Phys. Ed and Leadership at Lethbridge College, along with a few creative writing courses.

Eric was a natural fighter and was also excited about training with PFA, a gym in Lethbridge with one of his mixed martial arts mentors, Brad Wall (no relation to the Saskatchewan Premier).

Overall, it seemed everything was on track with Eric. To top that off, earlier in the year, he had found that special someone. Kathryn and Eric became immediately inseparable. Eric openly shared his past mental health struggles with Kathryn; he had an incredible honesty about him and she was also our family doctor's daughter. Sweet girl that she was, she accepted him for that.

Kathryn was also going to Lethbridge College in September and the two of them had both been accepted into the school's residence, so they were planning their fall and life of independence with great passion.

At the end of June, Eric quit his oil patch job to spend the summer working with personal training clients before heading to school.

It was as though the pieces of his life had come together beautifully.

Friday, August 2, Conner was in Saskatoon attending pilot training, and drove out to the family farm in Kenaston, where a rural country music festival hosted by my brother was going on. He was helping get everything ready. Eric was heading out on the six-hour drive to meet him there.

Eric had asked me if I wanted to go with him and had also texted a few friends to see whether they wanted to come. For one reason or another, we all declined. I told Eric I would go when I could enjoy the visit with family instead.

As he went to leave the house, we were talking about the drive he had ahead. I had a rosary in my hand that I had purchased for him. It was made by nuns in Ireland and I had found it in Calgary, at a convent where I often went to walk the labyrinth and sit in the peaceful gardens. I laughingly told him it was meant for him because of the Irish gene that made him crazy when he drank and asked if he wanted to take it along.

He just grinned at me and said, "No, Mom, I'm always losing shit like that." He asked again if I would go with him, and I again declined.

And that was it. A kiss, a hug, an "I love you," and he drove away in Justin's new black Ford F150 pick-up truck.

That memory is the last one I have of my son alive. It's a beautiful memory, tucked safely in my mother's grieving heart, where I can grab onto it when I need it most. Thank God for that beautiful final image of my son.

We spoke several times as he drove, and true to his word he texted me to let me know he had arrived.

"Hey Ma, I am home," was the message I received when he got to his grandmother's farm.

I replied "Ha Ha, you call it home, I still do too."

Our last communication.

It's funny how those last conversations stay anchored as you navigate through life in the fog of grief. Another fractured image from the day that changed my life forever.

4

Life Has Changed Forever

"I am only an arm's reach away from that next and lethal drink. I know that once I go there's no turning back. There's no knowing where I will go or what will happen."
—Eric Schmit

Coming Home

Although we made our home in Alberta for most of the younger two boys' lives, Kenaston would always be our true "home". Here, in mid-central Saskatchewan, was where both sides of the families lived and continue to live. It is where grandparents and great-grandparents had put down roots—as far back as the settlement of the province when the Dominion of Canada was giving away 160 acres of land to those brave souls who would make their way to the centre of this great land and try their hand at breaking and farming the prairie soil.

Kenaston, my home town, was largely populated by several families of Croatian descent from a tiny village in the former Yugoslavia, Lovinac. The community of individuals who moved to Canada in the hope of finding a better life was in many ways intact, and in so being, the culture of my father's familial heritage was also intact.

Eric loved the farm, his family, and the extended family which he found in Kenaston and nearby David-son where his father's family lived. In the year following his season in Washington state, he had gone to the farm to help my brother and while there stayed nearby with my mother. He wanted to train and save money so that he could go on more tryouts for his final year of junior hockey. He found the farm peaceful and calming, albeit lonely, as there were few people his age around. Just days before his death, when discussing the weekend ahead, he suggested he might stay at the farm for a few weeks and help out with harvest before getting ready to head to college. "The farm is always a good place to figure things out," he had said.

Sadly, instead of figuring things out, it was on the farm where he ended his life.

Eric often talked about the peace and serenity he found there. But that fateful night, peace and serenity eluded him. He instead walked the treed lane between the house and the barn, overlooking the hilly countryside, took his laces from his shoes, and, forming a noose, hanged himself from the tank where the farm fuel was stored.

The reasoning behind Eric's fated decision that night is something that only our imaginations can surmise, likely for the rest of our lives. There was nothing to indi-cate this would be the outcome of his long weekend in

Saskatchewan when he left home that Friday morning, or even in the hours preceding it.

If there was one truth that stood out about his struggle with mental illness and the highs and the lows, it was that the lows, when they hit, were fast and deep. A second truth is that alcohol fundamentally changed Eric's brain, not only fueling the depression but also making him impulsive and unpredictable. He had been drinking heavily the day of his death. He was taking mood-stabilizing medications. Perhaps the combination triggered something? Perhaps it was being surrounded by the safety of the farm and being encircled by family and friends, as ironic as that might sound? Perhaps he had simply grown weary of the highs, the lows and the in-betweens, which he had battled for so long.

Suicide is the most complex of sudden death experiences. Anyone who has lived through or been a bystander to a loved one's suicide knows without a shadow of a doubt that this is not a selfish act by an uncaring individual. Most often, the opposite is true: the person who felt compelled to take this final irrevocable measure to end their own pain was for the most part the kindest, most sensitive of souls, absorbing others' hurt and pain as though it were their own. This certainly was our Eric.

For reasons we will never know for certain, somewhere between 2:00 a.m., when the last person spoke to him, and 8:35 a.m., when my mother found him, my beautiful son lay down his sword, shook hands with the opponent he had waged war with for almost eight years, acknowledged he had given all he had and chose to search for whatever peace he might find in the next life that had eluded him for so long in this one.

And Then What?

Death such as this changes us. In an instant. Forever.

That's the face of tragedy.

How do you survive the death of a child? Or for my sons, the loss of your brother and best friend? I don't think you do survive. You exist. They—being those who have gone before on this difficult road—have shared the wisdom of their own experience of tragedy: that it doesn't get better, you simply learn to live with it. The first time I heard that particular statement, I didn't want it to be true. I remember thinking, in that moment of sheer panic, that if it didn't get better, I knew I could not live with this. Now, years later, caught somewhere between the timeless empty space which exists and the days which I have endured since Eric's death, I understand. And when I sadly have to share it with others beginning the journey of grief after tragic and unthinkable loss, I not only understand in my heart what that means, I also understand the reluctance reflected in the eyes of those with newly broken hearts to accept this reality.

The first days really were a haze. As a Catholic my entire life, and faithful follower of the church, I had always had a firm faith in the afterlife, believing that we are only here for a short while and then we cross over to a kinder, gentler existence where eternal rest and peace resides. It was that faith that I leaned on in the first few days. In many ways, I felt that the hand of God was very close to us.

Although we lived a province away, Eric had taken his life in our quiet little home village in Saskatchewan. We arranged for his funeral mass to be held in the same church he had been baptized in, and where his uncle and both grandfathers' funerals had been held. The funeral director had overseen every family funeral in our living family's history. He would be laid to rest right beside my father, nestled there with my ancestors, some of whom came to Canada more than a century ago.

These small communities rallied around us, both in Saskatchewan and Alberta. The church in Davidson (near Kenaston and his father's hometown) where the funeral mass was held was not only filled with lifelong friends of all of our families but overflowing with droves coming from Alberta.

The priest, although not having known Eric, spent the time required getting to know him through our stories. His sermon wasn't about a tragic early death, but of a beautiful soul who had finished his work on Earth and was called home.

"We look at this passing from our human eyes as a tragedy," he said. "But the truth is, from the moment we are born, we are old enough to die." How could we not feel comforted in spite of our loss?

One day, in between Eric's passing and the funeral, Conner and I drove between my mom's farm and his father's sister, Val's place. The autumn beauty of the prairie farm land—golden wheat fields, gravel roads, ditches filled with clover and long grass, and green sloughs—moved past us. As we drove, we spoke of how seeing his lifeless body proved the existence of a soul. The body that lay there barely resembled our beloved Eric. The sparkling eyes, the wit, the wisdom, the intelligent conversations—they left when he left us, of that we were certain.

"It's easy to believe in something when you have no reason not to," Conner said.

And I agreed. Despite our incredible sadness, we decided this proved there was another aspect of who we are that was more than the physical; that it was proof of an afterlife. We acknowledged that Eric was finally at peace, and that meant more than our devastating loss.

Send Me a Sign

Throughout those immediate days, I sought and found comfort in the smallest of signs that could confirm this afterlife.

My mother is very active in her church, and the faith community is strong in this little village. Somewhere between his death and the funeral, her closest friend

Agatha and another lady from the church came to visit. They brought a rosary and holy water, and the four of us went to the site where he had taken his life. As we said the rosary, I sent up a silent prayer.

Eric, please, please let me know you're okay.

The sun peaked out from the clouds.

"Nope," I whispered silently, "I need something better."

A small white butterfly flitted out from the native grasses growing alongside the dirt path. "Nope," I told him, "I need something better."

We got to the house, where I had left my iPhone on the kitchen table. I picked it up and there was a Facebook message. There was only the one, which was unusual as the messages hadn't stopped pouring in, in the brief hours since the news broke.

"Hi Joy!" it read. "You may or may not remember me, but I am the counsellor that Eric came to see a few times. I was very saddened to hear the news this morning about Eric passing away. The first thing I thought about was you. I remember him telling me how much he loved you. And also how much you pushed to help him. I will be thinking about you and your family."

"That's pretty good, Eric," I said through my tears, and replied to her that I had just prayed for an undeniable message from him. I felt I had received it.

"Joy, I am so happy that you received your undeniable message from Eric," the counsellor's message continued. "He was always so respectful, thoughtful and loving when he talked about you and his brothers. I am so sorry that I could not do more for him. I hope that you can find some peace in this, as I know that he would want that so desperately for you."

That day, that moment, that message, gave me the strength to put one foot in front of the other again.

His father and I were estranged and hadn't seen each other or spoken for years. The first time we saw each other post-divorce was outside of the same funeral home where his own brother and both our fathers had also been prepared for their final earthly journeys. As he got out of Justin's truck, any anger and resentment which previously existed from our difficult marriage was put away for both of us. The things that had once seemed so important paled in light of what we were now faced with: viewing the lifeless body of our precious middle son. We didn't speak. Sometimes there just aren't words that can ever capture the pain that is conveyed through eye contact and touch. He pulled out a tiny plastic Batman toy from a small white bag—his last gift for his Boogs.

Justin, Conner, their father and I, along with Justin's girlfriend Lisa, all made the horrible trip through the front door of the funeral home to face what we could no longer ignore.

Who went first? I don't remember. I do remember his father placing the toy in his lifeless, cold hand. And myself grasping the hand placed on his chest. His right foot kept falling to the side. He was so handsome, as always, in his custom-fitted suit, the coral shirt, and of course the black socks and his dress shoes.

Time will never erase from my memory the sight of his oldest brother Justin, the tough guy, collapsing to the floor, consumed with grief, with Conner's arms wrapped around him, tumbling down together. A single unit, they sobbed in a heap on the floor. As difficult as my own loss and immense pain were, they couldn't match being helpless to protect my other sons from this agonizing sorrow. Hours later, Kathryn arrived with her mother, Margaret. They had been on a pre-college visit to London, England when they received the news and made the horrific trip home across the Atlantic for Kathryn to have to come and face the same awful final visit.

From there, we stumbled through the motions of the days ahead. We decided on cremation, one reason being that we could keep small portions of his ashes—something that we wouldn't have realized if Conner hadn't thought to ask. His father and brothers kept three identical small urns, and we picked necklaces for Kathryn and I. Mine is never taken off except to shower or bathe. It goes with me everywhere—even through airport security.

The day before the funeral, his father, brothers and myself made the sad trip to the crematorium near Saskatoon. It's hard to describe how you keep moving forward as you chart this unknown territory, when everything in you is screaming at time to stop. In a daze, we entered the room where the cremation would take place. With each of us lifting at one of the hand holds of the cremation casket, the four of us placed the beautiful body of our precious Eric, plastic Batman in his hand, into the crematorium chamber. As the door slowly closed, Conner dropped to his knees his eyes unblinking so he could watch until it was impossible to see his beloved brother any more. Doug pressed the button to light the fire and begin the cremation. Together, we walked away, in silence, towards the vehicle and one step closer to the funeral service.

The next step was the prayer service traditionally held by many Christian denominations, including by Catholics, the night before the funeral. Following our personal journey through loss, I now believe this service also has another important function. It's a much-needed dry run, because nothing less can prepare you to walk into a funeral and the reality of what is ahead. It's so shocking and devastating.

That evening, together we walked to the front of the church. I recall from the days I worked with the Royal Canadian Mounted Police that black humour is a way of breaking up the overwhelming darkness of a moment. As we stood there with our arms around each other's shoulders, viewing the small urn that was now holding all that was left of our precious Eric, along with a framed picture beside it and some floral arrangements, Conner was the first to break the silence.

"And, weighing in at 2.75 ounces."

We all laughed, and then their father asked, "Do you think if we rub it, Eric will come back?"

We got through this first difficult passage, and memory once again clouds over until the following day. My mother and I went to the church early, and I sat outside in her SUV as I watched people enter for the funeral service. Even though Eric had never really lived here, the friends of both of our families seemed to all have made time to be there to support us, and one side of the church was filled just with the boys' friends and their families from Strathmore who had made the lengthy trip to be there as well. As we struggled to get through the pain-filled moments, we were surrounded by goodness and kindness that came from every corner of our lives.

My two remaining sons faced the biggest challenge of their lives in standing before this large crowd, delivering a joint eulogy. Justin shared the pain of falling asleep, crying and wanting to hold his little brother one last time. Both, in their words, invoked a challenge to all who gathered, about the honouring of Eric by imitating his goodness.

"When I woke up in the morning, I had a sense of calmness when I realized that, although we can no longer hold my brother in our arms, we can forever hold him in our hearts. The beautiful thing about the soul is that it will live on forever. We can hug Eric every time the sun shines on us, every time we hear a great song on the radio, and every time we reach out to a friend in need.

"People say they go to a funeral to pay their last respects. But you never have to pay 'last respects'. We can pay our respect to Eric every day, by living by the set of rules my brother lived with: treat every stranger as if they were your best friend, love unconditionally, never give up on your dreams, stand up for what is right and what you believe in."

Conner then told the story of how when Eric first passed away and they couldn't locate his phone, the brothers had made a pact that if they did find it, they would just keep the pictures and erase everything else.

"We weren't sure what we would find if we looked inside it, perhaps some answers. When we did find his phone, I'm so grateful we did look inside, because while we didn't find answers, what we found was the gift of Eric's words, and I'd like to share some of those with you today. These were written months before his death. May these, Eric's words, guide us all:

Recognizing my abilities as well as my flaws helps me become a better person.

To me, success has nothing to do with how much money you make. I want to be a spiritually successful person. I want to be liked, loved and respected by those I like, love and respect. Working as hard as I can, remaining confident, loving life and being passionate in everything I do is what I want. And that when the day comes and the man upstairs calls me up, I am surrounded by people who love me and will miss me, and when I arrive in the next world, I see Him, He puts his arm on my shoulder and says, "You did good, kid."

God, I pray I may find peace in my heart, harmony in my relationships and satisfaction in my goals. I pray I move along with reckless abandon and leave no one behind. I pray I make a positive impact on the world and may improve from pain as well as pleasure. I pray to find more love and friendship, for that is what I believe life is all about.

Instead of wishing for what I want, thank God for what I have.

St. Dymphna—Mental Illness

St. Raphael—Lovers

St. Sebastian—Athletes

St. Dymphna: *I humbly ask you, if you can, greet a message to God, that he may protect my mind with complete confidence and self-awareness. That when I fail, I may learn, and when I succeed, I may learn. Good St. Dymphna, I pray with you to the Lord.*

St. Sebastian: *I pray with you that I may have the faith and confidence to remain a competitor and I may always be strong in body and mind, which allows me to be a successful Mixed Martial Artist.*

St. Raphael: *I pray I may find the friendship and love of trusting friends and lovers. I pray that no one gets hurt in my relationships with them, whether they be friends or lovers. I pray I be true as well as they.*

Another special piece of the funeral was the song that ended the ceremony. I had a cousin whose daughter, Angie, had the most remarkable gift. Although she had multiple surgeries as a newborn to try to save her sight, she was declared legally blind. However, this had been compensated for with not only an ear that could hear every single tone and pitch, but a voice that could replicate it. I had asked if she would sing a special song for Eric. It was called *Arms of Heaven*, a song about a child dying, written by a good friend of mine, Kenny Munshaw.

> *There's a child tonight in the arms of heaven,*
> *Taken early from the garden of his life.*
> *And the grass grows green where he's resting,*
> *Watered gently by the hands of those he loved.*
> *But do the tears we cry change the way we live?*
> *No one sees inside, but our hearts they won't give.*
> *And I hope and pray, we will meet some day,*
> *Once again in the arms of Heaven.*

Kenny sent the music and Angie's lovely voice wrapped up the funeral mass.

The mass now completed, the next difficult stage was the burial. Kenaston was approximately 20 miles from Davidson, where his funeral mass had been held. I remember, as the funeral procession made its way to Kenaston, looking in the rear-view mirror, and as far as the eye could see, a steady stream of vehicles followed to take Eric to his final resting spot, safe with my father, his beloved Grandpa George.

Although fractured mere days before, our family was completely united in how we honoured Eric. We were now bound by something far greater: shared loss. We participated as a single entity in every step. At the grave-side, we laid white roses as a bed in the small hole where his urn full of ashes would be laid, held in a green satin bag. We then took turns placing small gifts. I lowered the rosary he had left with me in Strathmore. I don't recall what the others did, but each of us placed a piece of our hearts there with him. His friends then took their turns leaving small gifts with Eric. We laid the first and final scoops of dirt. A lovely spray of yellow roses in a hand-made arrangement from a friend from Strathmore was the final touch.

5

My Fractured Self,
and the Search Begins

"Never let me lose faith."
—Eric Schmit

Search for Meaning Begins

In Deepak Chopra's book, *God: A Story of Revelation*, he looks at the meaning or concept of God from 10 different faiths or spiritual perspectives, with stories that range from Job to Socrates to St. Paul, all the way to Rabindranath Tagore. In the chapter that looks at the spiritual journey of Rumi, a medieval Muslim poet, he articulates a plausible conversation between Rumi and his spiritual guide, Shams. In this story, Shams uses a candle as the tool for which to pose the question about God's light.

Rumi answers the question with a question. "But the light of God isn't the same as ordinary light. If the candle burns out, can you say that God has disappeared?"

To this, Shams replies "God disappears all the time. When people lose a child or their money or all their sheep, in my experience, they usually lose God."

That was my experience. And it is a stage consistent with the processing of trauma—the loss of belief systems and identity. In losing Eric, God had disappeared from my life. The light had indeed gone out, and in this new darkness I lost everything that had ever made sense to me. All that had once been sacred to me, whether my faith or even my identity as a mother, had been shaken to the core of my being. I didn't even know who I was anymore.

And so, I began a desperate and relentless search for answers about life, lives lived, the afterlife, the mystery of life and death. The same questions that had confounded humans since time immemorial were now my questions too.

The first days and the immediacy of the funeral behind me, as the awful reality set in, I began to reflect, analyze, over-analyze and grieve ceaselessly. Where once a simple unquestioned faith resided now was an open chasm of pain desperately needing answers.

The evening of the funeral, I wanted to go back to Alberta—to be home. It was as though I desperately needed to flee all the pain that I had experienced in the past few days, and I wanted to run from it in the only direction I knew. The same flight mechanism that Eric exhibited in times of stress found a home in my psyche.

At 9:30 that night, I frantically began packing and getting myself ready to drive. My poor mother just watched helplessly as I got everything together. Conner was in the same state. But for whatever reason, we decided to wait until the next day to make the trip and I fell into bed, aided by the sleeping pills that would become, over the next several months, my constant companion and only escape from the pain of the day and fear of the next.

I drove Justin's truck back to Alberta, the same one Eric had driven out to Saskatchewan. I stopped at the cemetery for one last visit to his gravesite.

The August sun was hot on the prairies in the summer. The sky was blue, with a mixture of puffy white cumulus clouds and wispy cirrus clouds spread across the vastness. I threw myself on the ground, hugging his grave, my face buried in the flowers. I could feel the heat of the sun on the black dirt as I gave in to the torrent of tears.

Eventually, I rolled onto my back and stared at the sky, as though somehow the emptiness held the answers.

"Where are you, my Eric?" I wondered.

Then, laying there in my heartbreak, tears rolling down my face, looking Heavenward, I acknowledged that despite the pain of the loss, had I known the heartbreak which lay ahead, had I been given the choice to still have Eric in my life knowing he would leave early, I would have chosen the gift of Eric, even for a short while. The pain of loss was nothing compared to the joy he had brought by his too-short presence in my life. This perspective settled deep into my heart and I finally found the strength to leave his graveside—all I had left of him—and begin the trip home.

Afterlife Communications

As I left the cemetery, I again desperately asked Eric to give me a sign.

In the aftermath of this tragic loss—as Shams had even used in his example to Rumi—God had gone from a defined loving presence in a home where we aspired to meet him and our departed loved ones in joyful reconciliation, to an unfathomable mystery, the solving of which consumed my waking (and sleeping) hours. What proof, really, did we have that life goes on?

As I put miles behind me, I remembered how in our last phone conversation, as he drove out, Eric had told me how easily he was driving the truck. And so, taking my cue from that memory, I slowly made my way home, not hurrying. I listened to his iPod. His favourite music connected me to him and brought me a combined sorrow and comfort as I drove, completely alone, immersed in my thoughts.

Several of Conner's friends who had driven out at once upon learning of Eric's death were also on their way back to Strathmore. As I passed through the intersection of the two highways leaving town, they saw me driving alone and immediately called to see if I needed company for the ride. I assured them I would be fine, that this was a drive I needed to make on my own.

The boys and I had a route we always drove between Strathmore and Kenaston. It was a secondary highway that paralleled one of the main thoroughfares. It became our main route throughout the years, as it was in great condition and had very little traffic.

As I drove, I reflected. I watched the prairie sky and marveled in the beauty of nature as the hot summer sun and blue skies guided me westward. Throughout the entire drive, I waited desperately for a sign from Eric. The fear of there possibly being no more than the here and now took my breath away in panic. And within these moments of the panic, I would find myself searching once again for a sign to give me hope and keep me going. I kept thinking I would get something about three—the three inseparable brothers would be marked in some way as my message from Eric. But there wasn't any sign. No three eagles, nothing.

I had just gone through the Drumheller Valley, a winding historic part of the badlands of east-central Alberta, when I received a text message from a medium who I had seen a few times before. I hadn't contacted her since Eric had died. She could have only been aware of his death from the numerous messages on my Facebook page.

"Joy, I have Eric here with me," the text said. "He wants you to listen to the song *My Immortal* by Evanescence."

I replied that I was driving but I would check it when I got to the house, as I wasn't far from home. Which, of course, was a lie. I had found and was already listening to the song before I'd replied. Music had always been an important part of our family. I loved the eclectic music the boys introduced to me, the country music enthusiast. This song wasn't one that I had heard of.

She texted me back, "You're texting and driving! Don't do that!" followed by a second text. "Eric just said, 'She won't listen anyhow.'"

I listened to the words, which were beautifully reflective of Eric's earthly struggles—phrases such as "I'm so tired of being here," and "These wounds won't seem to heal" couldn't have been more accurate.

But there was another line that didn't make sense. "When you cried, I'd wipe away all of your tears."

Just as I thought to myself, "I don't understand, I don't get this, Eric," she immediately texted again.

"He says, 'Mom you couldn't fix me. This wasn't you. It wasn't your fault. You held my hand, you wiped my tears.'"

There were a few more messages, and then a final, "He says, 'Ha ha, Mom, you always take the back roads. Don't hurry.'"

There was so much about this that made sense. I felt somehow that Eric had reached across the veil to make sure I had a message that let me know how close he still was to all of us.

I don't remember getting home that evening, or where Conner and Justin were. I remember how scared though I was to stay alone in that empty house. Fortunately, my good friends took turns staying with me through the first awful nights, as I slowly adapted to the newfound emptiness in a house that had only days before been so alive with the three boys and their antics and activities.

The following morning was a whirlwind, as this was the day of the second service. When we had planned Eric's funeral mass in Saskatchewan, I remember that we discussed needing something in Strathmore as well, and my response that I didn't want to bury my son in a school. Although I had gone to mass in the school gymnasium in the years since our church had been condemned, and the boys had gone through their elementary years to graduation in the building, it seemed unthinkable to me that this was where we would hold his funeral.

I need not have worried, though. I barely recall that during the planning process in Saskatchewan, while meeting with the funeral director, I had received a message from one of the girls he had gone to high school with. One of a set of twins who had been his friends—Kayla or Kendra, I can't remember which—in the fog of the early days, had asked if they could help by planning something in Strathmore. I had told them it was a great idea. The girls' father was the minister of the local Alliance church. The energy of Eric's many friends was poured into honouring him with their own beautiful church service, hosted at the Alliance church. Once again, the hand of God seemed to be with us.

As we arrived for the service that afternoon, people crushed around all of us as we tried to make our way in, reaching out, hugging and holding us as they shared their genuine grief at our loss. The minister had to come outside and take us down to the basement, where there was a waiting room. The flow of people into the church was such that the ushers eventually gave up and were forced to quit seating people, and were unable to hand out the funeral cards.

Other than the eulogy his brothers delivered, the same one they had shared at his mass, and the final song, *Take Your Candle, Go Light Your World*, where we as family started a light from a single candle and turned the church into a room of lit candles as we walked out to the song, the entire service was coordinated and orchestrated by Eric's friends. It was beautiful, and then they shared a meal—again completely put together by friends and volunteers and enough to feed this massive crowd.

The line-up to speak to me was over three hours long, and most people endured the wait. I needed to honour every single person who came, who shared and who grieved with us. There were many who later told me they just spoke to his brothers and father and left rather than wait in the lineup. When I stopped by the church after a few days, the minister told me that Eric's funeral was the largest event he had ever held in the building, with even the overflow packed.

There is this common wisdom that somehow you stumble through the funeral (in our case, funerals) and then this is where the awful reality sets in as everyone slowly leaves and other lives go back to normal. I don't recall much about those next weeks. My work had arranged grief counselling, and our lives continued to be filled with acts of kindness and love from the community we had called home for 15 years. There was a steady stream of visitors for days after we returned home.

Just prior to Eric's death, I had been working on a special project called the Calgary Poverty Reduction Initiative, a citywide initiative looking at how to identify and then address the key factors influencing poverty in the city. There were two findings that I reflected on in the days following his death: firstly, how broad the swath of vulnerability was, and secondly, how important community was in surviving tragedy and finding resiliency. Within days of the final report being filed with the City of Calgary, the co-chair of the initiative lost his home in the mass flooding Calgary saw in late June, and six weeks later I lost my son. When I came back to work, we had a quiet lunch together, and reflected on the irony of this. There were many days when I questioned how others survived such tragedy and loss without the kind of support we had experienced. I wonder that to this day. Our family, our friends, and our community held us up during our darkest hour. They still do.

Beer?

One cannot have a conversation about the life-changing impact of trauma without looking at the concept of time and how it is altered. For the individual, the world stands still, and there is confusion as to how the rest of the world continues to go on around you. The minutes you think you can't possibly survive eventually turn into hours, which somehow turn into days. You count them all. Life becomes, for the first while, "X" amount of days since he died, since our lives changed forever. And then, time as we have previously understood it doesn't really exist at all. However, certain calendar events give a framework of sorts to the journey.

The first time I went back to Kenaston was on the September long weekend, Labour Day in Canada, a month following his passing. Not only did I want to spend time with my mother, but I also needed to go back to visit Eric's graveside. My friend and neighbour Tracey, who, with her family, had been at our sides throughout the entire journey from the beginning of symptoms to the final difficult end, wanted to come with me, for the same reasons.

As I waited for her, I picked up a book, one of many I had purchased as I struggled to come to terms with this new question about the mystery of life and death. It was called *Hello from Heaven*, and it was a collection of short stories of signs people had received from their loved ones who died. One set of stories stood out in the simple testimonials of connection. These were about smells that people had experienced in the time after a death. I didn't think much of it, and as soon as Tracey was ready, I headed over to pick her up.

It was a difficult drive home, and my anxiety level was extremely high. We ended up leaving Strathmore late, so by the time we got to Kenaston, it was already dark. We pulled up to the gates of the cemetery and unloaded our treasures: flowers, a luminary to light his gravesite, and several gifts friends had sent, including a teddy bear and a silver necklace with a cross. We laid them on the ground in the darkness.

Harvest was now in full swing and the evening was cool, but not cold, typical of autumn in Saskatchewan. I said a few prayers, shed a few tears and Tracey and I laughed at a can of beer that someone had left on the right-hand side of my father's headstone, obviously for Eric. I silently wondered if he and Grandpa might have to wrestle for that one.

Situated across Highway 11, east from the actual town site of Kenaston, the cemetery is shielded by a row of evergreen trees to the west, planted by some forward-thinking community members years before.

The access to the cemetery is less than 50 metres off Highway 15 and on a gravel road. As we pulled away from the cemetery gate and onto the gravel road, I clearly smelled beer. Which was impossible, because I didn't drink, and my car was only months old. As we went to turn east onto the highway to my mother's farm, I turned to Tracey.

"I smell beer."

Tracey looked at me and said in equal surprise, "Me too. I just didn't want to say anything because I thought maybe it was a farm smell and I didn't know."

And as soon as we acknowledged it, the smell was gone, as abruptly as it had come. I burst out laughing. Only Eric would send me the smell of beer to let me know he was near! It was one of our arguments, or the source of our only arguments. I was the beer hunter in our "dry house." I could walk in the door and know if someone had been drinking. Alcohol and its misuse had been something that had affected my entire life, so much so that I was hyper vigilant to any indication someone near me was drinking. If this was an afterlife communication, Eric had picked something I couldn't deny as a gift to communicate to me from the other side.

That was the first trip back to Saskatchewan, and the second trip home. So much had changed; at the top of the list was my faith and my perception of life in general. When my father had passed away after his long battle with cancer, he was ready. "I've had a good run" he would say. It was easy to believe that he had gone to a kinder, gentler world. With Eric's death, faith in the afterlife was proving to be the hardest thing in the world for me to find.

Every moment of each day, I obsessed over where he was—if anywhere. What did it look like where he was now? Was he okay? Where was he? Was there something more? Or maybe not? The questions ran endlessly through my mind. Although I had always struggled with sleep, the racing thoughts were relentless and the only way I could escape was through the use of sleeping pills to block the thoughts. I knew if I didn't rest, I wouldn't survive.

By the third week after Eric's death, I could feel myself slipping into my own depression and pit of hopelessness. Within a month, I was back to work; I saw it as preserving my own sanity by being able to throw myself into something that could divert my thoughts even momentarily from the pain that ate away at me in my waking hours.

Where Does Faith Go?

The church I had previously attended every Sunday in Strathmore now became unthinkable. I couldn't seem to come to terms with mass in a school gymnasium, especially in the school where my sons' memories were lurking in every hallway, nook and cranny. In addition to desperately needing anonymity in my grief, I also felt I needed a message of hope. The priest, although judicious in his following of the Roman Catholic faith, had a more rigid view of faith, or God, and of life than what I personally did. Before losing Eric, it hadn't seemed significant, and I attended mass out of a sense of obligation.

In the aftermath, I knew I needed far more, and decided I was going to do some God shopping.

One night during my first week back at work, I deviated slightly from my usual drive home because of construction, and I passed a church called Mary Mother of the Redeemer. I felt the urge to pull in, as I'd always had a connection to Mary. Although it was after their posted work hours, I drove into the parking lot and tried the door. It was unlocked. The church secretary, fortunately, was still on site, and as I tearfully explained to her why I had stopped, she called the priest.

We sat and talked, and I poured out my heart to him. About the walk through my son's mental illness, about the current fragility of my faith, and even my own lack of will to live, but needing to for my other two sons. He was the gentlest of men. As a chaplain at the hospital, he said he dealt with the dying, but also with individuals with mental illness. He explained to me how mental illness turns the brain upside down when it cycles, and how it was so often the disease of intelligent, sensitive individuals. He had so aptly just described my son. He explained to me how it was our human nature to fight to live, how as we died we were struggling until our last breath to remain. Yet, for those with mental illness, when they had chosen to take their lives, it was because their pain was so great that they couldn't stay. That, he said, proved that mental illness was truly in contrast to what our wellness as humans looked like, validating it as a medical condition. In doing so, he gave me peace that the church I had once followed and now feared judgment from in my son's suicide showed itself to be one of compassion and kindness.

We talked about the fragility of my faith.

"I can't be angry at God," I said. "I've never been angry or felt that that this was somehow a road more difficult than others would walk. I just don't understand. I can't make sense of any of this, and what I've once believed doesn't seem to be so easy to believe anymore."

"That," he said, "is why it is called faith. Because faith by its definition isn't something that we can prove. We simply have to believe."

And belief, he assured me, didn't necessarily come easy. He explained that I was not alone in questioning my faith. Many well-known biblical and religious figures struggled as well with their faith, he said, citing Job in the Bible, Saint Paul and Mother Theresa. Each of these had asked many times, "Why?" and struggled to come to terms with the meaning of this pain-filled earthly life. He told me that eventually, I would have to give up on trying to solve the mystery of life and death, that it is called a mystery for the reason that no one has ever been able to explain it.

He let me look inside the church. I instantly felt at home and made the decision that this lovely church would become my new parish. I felt doubly blessed that this church was not only Mary Mother of the Redeemer, but had previously been known as Our Lady of Grace parish. It felt like home to me.

Throughout my lifetime, imbedded deep in my Catholicism, I had had a special affinity to Mary, the Blessed Virgin. We shared a birthdate of September 8, and Eric was born on the anniversary of the Miracle of Fatima, October 13. The Holy Rosary was specific to the Catholic faith and is how we experience Christ through Mary. Our connection to Mary was further evidenced in the custom the boys and I had adopted in bringing rosaries to each other and to my mother. My mother, to this day, says the rosary each morning for whoever has given her that particular one.

When Eric had travelled to the Vatican as part of his high school Europe trip for Easter, he brought me back a stunning rosary. It was constructed of beads made from deep red stones with dark grey in the marbling and held together by a thicker metal, with *Vaticano* embossed in the centerpiece. As he gave it to me, he explained that when he was asking the woman for help in choosing a rosary for his mother, she brought him several white ones to pick from. But he said he saw this one and he knew this was the one he wanted for me.

"I picked it because it was strong, Mom, just like you."

I cherished this rosary. Unfortunately, because of its beauty and because of how much it meant to me, I kept it in my purse in its small gold gift bag so that I could do my daily rosary on it as I drove the one-hour commute to work in Calgary. One day, as I reached in to get it, I realized in horror that it had fallen out of my purse. I couldn't find it anywhere. I retraced my steps to the stores I had been to that day and left my phone number everywhere with the promise of a reward.

I spoke to the building security guard about it, and he mentioned that he had seen it on the ground of the parking lot I used at the time, right beside the building where I worked. I ran outside in a vain hope that it would still be there. It wasn't. I saw three homeless people sitting on a tree branch beside my car. I explained to them not only my loss, but that my son had been sick and that this rosary was very precious to me. The two men and one woman looked intently at me as they listened to my story. The man on the left reached around his neck and took off a chain he was wearing. It was a St. Christopher medal that had been given to him by a priest at the Catholic Centre just blocks away. He held it out to me and said, "I want you to have this, to keep you safe."

I couldn't accept it, but I was profoundly humbled by the experience. This man, living on the streets, was willing to give to me one of the few things he had and held dear. The rosary never did reappear, although I think of it almost daily. Perhaps whoever found it needed the strength and inspiration of their own faith renewed.

When Conner went to the Vatican the following year, he brought me another rosary, blessed by the Pope. While Eric brought me a rosary that represented strength to him, Conner brought me one that represented beauty, with ornate intricate silver patterns to hold black beads in place. This was the one I had used in prayer the morning I learned of Eric's death.

In Eric's passing, although I knew it was a common response to tragedy, the one emotion I couldn't connect to was anger towards God as I understood him to be. Hadn't God also lost his son? As for the Blessed Virgin, she too had watched her son struggle and die. I knew that the burden I was bearing was no more than the burden we believed in our own faith that our Heavenly Father and Blessed Mother also carried. I never asked, "Why me?" Because I knew the answer to that was, "Why not me?"

Each of us somehow, throughout our life, has to deal with something at some point that will seem far bigger than our capacity to carry it. This was mine.

It was the carrying it that I struggled with. My "Why?" was about life in general, about the meaning of the suffering that was part of the human experience. This was where my faith was challenged in Eric's death. What could possibly be the meaning of all of this pain we endure here on Earth if there was indeed more to life than this?

As difficult as it was to connect to my faith, it was also all I had to connect to. If I could find faith again, hope again, I could learn to accept this loss and connect back to life. But I knew this was going to be far easier said than done, given the state of my shattered soul.

The Illusion of Normalcy

By this point, the days had now rolled into weeks. Although we still marked time by days—37 days since Eric had died, 52 days since Eric had died—time was marching on. I'm not exactly sure when our marker became weeks, though. And then months.

Justin and Eric had fought together for several years in mixed martial arts competitions, acting as corner men for each other. At the time of Eric's death, he had been scheduled to fight in Weyburn, SK and Justin was to fight at a King of the Cage Canada main event in Medicine Hat, AB. The two cities were about a six-hour drive apart. Eric had been worried because he didn't know how he could meet his weigh-in at Weyburn and then make it back to Justin's fight, so he could corner for him that night.

Other than his first two fights in Mexico, Justin had never fought without Eric there. They trained together endlessly and often Conner would join them as a sparring partner. Conner had never missed a fight, although he wasn't personally interested in the competitive aspects of the sport.

Eric's death was crushing in more ways than there are words to write, but Justin fighting someone in the main event, mere weeks after Eric's passing, a top fighter whom he had previously met in the ring, was extremely stressful.

There was significant media leading up to the event, including some promotional videos that had been filmed while Eric was still alive. He had been at the filming with Justin. To have Justin fight in his grieving state terrified us all.

When I got there, my neighbour Tracey handed me Justin's rosary. She said he had waited for me until he had to go change and had asked her to hand it to me as soon as I arrived. The rosary had been a gift I had given him for his birthday; it was called the *Stairway to Heaven* rosary.

As in their childhood, my inability to watch my children hurt formed a pattern for when the boys fought. Since I couldn't bring myself to be present, I would leave the arena when I knew they were going to fight—in both hockey and in mixed martial arts. However, I usually had a plan so that someone texted me updates so I would know when everything was finished, and I would be able to go back to the event.

That night, Conner was white with worry, terrified he might lose his only remaining brother. Forgetting to ask anyone to keep me in the know, I leapt from the stands after Justin walked into the cage to Eric's fight song, "A Call to Arms" by 30 Seconds to Mars. I headed out the doors of the arena, into the night and to the parking lot where I paced up and down the rows of cars in the dark. There I was, holding Justin's rosary in my hand and talking out loud, looking up to the sky, begging Eric with everything I had to watch out for his brother. To be in his corner. Because I had forgotten to ask anyone to message me updates, I was tormented by the silence from inside the arena.

Suddenly, I heard, "Mom! Mom!" and turned, my heart racing. I saw Conner leap over the rails of the entrance doors with his arms in the air. Justin had won his fight—the main event. We raced back to the stands together and I was able to get down to the fighters' area to give my son a huge hug. Tears were flowing freely. The whole section was filled with teary-eyed people hugging and kissing. For those who didn't know the magnitude of this fight from an emotional perspective, it must have seemed like a severe overreaction in the name of sport.

We went to the after party to have a quick bite to eat and then head back to Strathmore, which meant a 4 a.m. arrival home.

Along the way, Tracey sent me a message. "Did you see that picture of Justin and Conner in the ring?"

I replied I had and didn't think much more of it at the time.

The next morning, coffee in hand, I began to scan the Facebook posts from the night before. As I saw one, there was an undeniable violet haze in a cloud-like form centred above Justin and Conner in the ring post-fight. This was the one my neighbour had messaged me about. I immediately Googled what purple meant in spirituality and learned that it was representative of a message from Heaven from a deeply loving soul. I saw that Al, the friend who had taken and posted the photo, was online, so I messaged him. He said that when he been in the ring with Justin and Conner he had an overwhelming sense of Eric being there with them and couldn't shake it. When he posted the pictures, he said, "Eric" was there in every single one and he sent me several other images, all with this strange purple haze floating above the two.

To my mother's grieving heart, everything was a message. This one seemed especially so.

However, we all grieve differently. As I sought out these messages of hope and healing and love, his brothers were less inclined to believe so. In fact, they were increasingly irritated by my connecting everything back to Eric.

Justin, in his frustration, replied back to me. "Not everything is a message from Eric, Mom. He isn't a flying purple messenger from God. He is the dead kid. He obviously wanted to go, so let him rest in peace. Please," he begged me.

Conner, like Justin, was weary of my need to find evidence of Eric in every situation, but he was less vocal in admonishing me.

That's been one of the hardest parts of the loss, knowing that each of us has to come to terms with sorrow in our way. And realigning not only your family, but your entire belief system, does not come easy, no matter where you think you started.

6

Living the Trauma Effect

"The air is always cold and it seems thick in October. Especially in Canada, but in Washington too, it was a certain kind of cold, the one that reminds you that it's going to stay for awhile."
—Eric Schmit

The Sorrowful Firsts

There is a common wisdom about the sorrowful firsts of everything. What would have been Eric's 21st birthday was approximately nine weeks after his death. We were all still struggling to grasp even breathing without him, much less how to acknowledge the date of his birth. Another Strathmore hockey mom had lost her son three years before Eric, also to suicide. She was a source of great comfort during these early days, and more importantly, she imparted gentle wisdom about what to expect. She advised that the days leading up to it would be harsher and more emotional than the day of.

And so, the days leading up until October 13 were filled with trepidation and sadness. Not that the days prior hadn't been, but somehow trying to anticipate how to deal with what had always been the happiest of happy days suddenly seemed hard to comprehend.

Eric's graveside was a tangible place for me to visit him. We—Conner and I—decided to go to Kenaston for the Thanksgiving weekend. Eric had been born the day after Thanksgiving, and so his birthday often fell on the holiday. I had a mass said for Eric that day, but other than that, there is little I remember about the trip there, or back to Strathmore. It was getting late and his friends were waiting to also mark Eric's birthday with us. Many had gone to college in September, including Eric's girl-friend Kathryn.

When I got to the house, I was greeted by the presence of a bouquet of helium balloons all decorated with Batman insignia. It was well past supper and I ran to the grocery store to ensure there was food for Eric's friends when they arrived. As I breezed through Sobeys, I wondered, "Do we get a cake?" I really couldn't decide if this would be right or wrong. In hindsight, I know there are no rights or wrongs when you grieve. I decided to purchase a Batman cake, and then ran to pick up Kathryn, who brought a tray of her homemade chocolate cupcakes that she used to make for Eric.

When we got back to the house, the rest of his friends were already there and we loaded the latest Batman movie. Again, memory is vague, and the evening was far too emotional.

We had always had a rule in my home, following the divorce. I wanted a "dry" house, meaning there would be no alcohol. My life had been marked by the trauma, the confusion, and the pain that comes with alcohol use and abuse. It wasn't always followed, but it was the only rule I really had. Eric's friends were, of course, usually respectful of that, especially this night in particular.

However, my own family, in their own grief, didn't honour this rule. It was the final straw in an already emotionally charged day. In front of Eric's friends, I broke down, screaming at them for disrespecting what I wanted; especially when it was the one thing that I could point to that had caused Eric to take his life. The way alcohol affected his brain functioning meant we never knew what he might do, and it was always something completely unpredictable. Had he not been drinking that night, I believed Eric would still have been with us.

Eric's friends, shocked by my outburst, were regardless very supportive. We left the movie playing and I drove some of the kids home, including Kathryn.

I went over to a friend's house and got a few hours of good sleep. At some time during the early morning, I received a text message from my cousin Ray, that his wife died peacefully at home with her family at her side.

Conner was leaving with his father for Australia the next morning. I didn't see him before they left. I picked Kathryn up in the morning, as she lived close to my friend's house. We arrived home, and our neighbours, the Molina family who had left the helium balloons, came over. We gathered around the island in the kitchen and all wrote messages to Eric. We tied them to the balloons and made a bouquet. Marcus, our neighbour's son, was only eight at the time. He had been experiencing a terribly difficult time in dealing with losing Eric. The last time he had seen him had been at his own birthday party just weeks before.

There was a park slightly over a block from our house. Eric had spent a summer landscaping and that park had been one of the projects he had worked on. Not only that, but when he was personal training, he would often take his clients to the park, which bordered on a small lake, and would work with them there. It seemed the fitting place to release the balloons.

Marcus jumped up on a large rock that was part of the landscape and sent the balloons Heavenward. We all watched the balloons float higher and higher and followed them until they were a tiny speck, and then completely invisible. Of all the things we had tried to do, this seemed to be the most successful and meaningful way to acknowledge the day the gift of Eric had entered our lives.

We now had one difficult first behind us.

The First Dream

I'm not sure when the first dream of Eric happened. Every night, as I laid down for sleep, I prayed for a dream, a sign of some kind from my son. I felt the only way left to connect with him—if there really was a here-after—was to have him bring me a message in a dream. I needed this confirmation there was something more, but more importantly that he was safe. It was like when I took the each of the boys to kindergarten for the first time. I would watch from the door and then through the windows of their classrooms, making sure they were okay. Except now there wasn't a window for me to look into, to give me that comfort that he was okay.

Justin said that it felt like when you're waiting at the airport for your loved one to walk through the doors, that sense of anticipation or excitement. Whichever it was, we were all waiting for something to give us a sign that there was indeed a place for Eric to be where he was safe, and free from the stress that this world had placed on his gentle heart.

The dream came, although there weren't a lot of words. The little I remember is that Eric was transparent, for lack of a better explanation. He was smiling and happy. He told me he was worried about my health, and that I needed to take more supplements. Then I asked him how I would know he was near, what the sign would be, and he laughed and said, "Think of cherry tree blossoms, Mom."

And he was gone.

And I remember, in my frustration, saying, "Eric, where am I going to find cherry tree blossoms?"

The next day, when I went to work, I received a beautiful Facebook message from a friend, with a message about a broken heart on a background of cherry tree blossoms. And a few hours later, I received a thank you card from a work colleague. The image on the front was a cherry tree in full blossom, with silver sparkles across it.

Okay, Eric, I promise I will know you're close whenever I see cherry tree blossoms.

The Unexpected Physical Side of Grief

It seemed Eric's worry about my health was legitimate.

Prior to his passing, Eric had been my personal trainer and had given me the perfect program to manage stress while being a single parent, working full time and doing my Masters' degree, all at the same time. I loved weightlifting; if anything, I over-trained. He and his brothers would caution me to not train so hard, that there was a point where it became counter-productive, as my body needed time to recover.

In the days following Eric's death, I immediately threw myself back into the gym, at times training up to two hours a night. Unfortunately, as I had no appetite, I wasn't compensating for the additional demands on my body. I had also typically suffered from migraines. Calgary has been known to be one of the worst places in Canada for migraine sufferers because of the rapid barometric pressure shifts that come with the chinooks—warm Pacific air blowing over the Rocky Mountains.

Although my health seemed to be holding up, there were cracks in my wellness. I was losing weight and my migraines were increasing. But I couldn't stop going to the gym. It was the only place other than sleep where I could find any kind of relief from my overwhelming pain.

I went to the local hospital emergency in early October for what seemed at the time a typical migraine. My vasodilator medications hadn't worked and the pain and accompanying nausea were so severe I needed to be given a morphine/metoclopramide combination intravenously until the symptoms abated. Once treated in hospital to get the pain under control, I could be released to go home and rest. Having had migraines for years, this was a pattern the local hospital and I were well accustomed to.

It was within days that I had to go to Ottawa, where my old friend Laureen Harper—the wife of the then Prime Minister—was co-chairing an event for youth mental health called The Kaleidoscope of Hope. She had invited me within days of Eric's passing, but also wondered if it would be too early for me to come. I had decided this was something I was going to face head-on, and so immediately replied that I wanted to attend, and that Kathryn would like to accompany me.

As we were flying to Ottawa, I experienced unbearable pain in my sinuses. By the time we landed, I had symptoms of a terrible cold—even though I hadn't had one when we left Calgary.

Throughout the next day, I was still very sick but managed to pull it together for the gala event. While there, we met the entertainers as well as many families who had been impacted by their children's mental health challenges, including those who had lost loved ones. One family in particular stood out to both Kathryn and I; they seemed so much "like us". Their son, an athletic, gentle child in a loving family, who seemed to have everything going for him, had ended his life several years prior. Their compassion and empathy were something that touched me deeply. The father was one of the speakers at the event and he said to me the one bit of advice he could impart that I would also hear over and over again: it doesn't get better; you simply learn to live with it.

That seemed unfathomable to me at the time. I didn't know how I could ever learn to live with this crushing grief.

It was at this event where I met Robb Nash, of The Robb Nash Project. Robb himself had been in a near fatal car accident in his teens. Following a long and difficult recovery, he became one of the country's top musical acts, Live on Arrival. However, after a while, he questioned what he was doing with his own second chance at life and, leaving the world of public stardom behind, began taking a message of hope to vulnerable youth in schools, prisons, detention centres and addiction treatment programs across the country. We spoke a few times over the course of the night and Robb gave me a card to connect with his scheduler back in Calgary, so I could attend one of these shows.

Over the next few days in Ottawa, Kathryn and I managed to fit in some sightseeing and some visits with family and friends. But for the most part, I spent huge amounts of time in bed, trying to get the upper hand on this cold that had hit so harshly and suddenly. I felt so awful, as I had wanted to show Kathryn the city. Eric, Conner and I had visited many times and it was a place that held many special memories.

One day, we ventured out to Harrington Lake, the Prime Minister's official summer residence, where Eric and I had visited in 2007 during one of our trips to Ottawa. At the guesthouse, Kathryn and I looked around a bit and she opened the guest book. It fell open to Eric's and my guest entry, of all pages. It seemed he was there with us.

After our short visit, Kathryn's parents picked us up at the airport and, being that her father David was our family physician, I got in to see him right away. He put me on antibiotics for a sinus infection. I had not had an infection of any kind, or been on medication other than for my migraines, since Conner was a baby. David explained to me that grief was like a serious physical illness and that it would take time, likely at least a year, for me to begin feeling like myself again just physically.

Over the next few months, I was back and forth to the doctor and placed on increasingly stronger courses of antibiotics. The infection was resistant to healing. My other two sons were extremely worried about me, but with Justin away working and Conner away at school, they could only watch and worry from a distance.

As I struggled with my ongoing health issues, particularly the sinus infection that simply wouldn't let up, and the migraines that seemed to go hand in hand, I happened to be discussing it with a co-worker and friend. She shared that when her daughter had been going through cancer treatment, she herself had also been plagued with a reoccurring and debilitating sinus infection.

Whether it was family wisdom or medical knowledge this was based on, she couldn't recall, but she had been advised that the grieving often find that they experience this infection. I didn't know the science behind it, but it seemed to make sense, the sinuses being so close to our tear ducts, that tears or the repression of tears could indeed be why ongoing sinus infections were one of the outcomes of the grief experience. It certainly made sense to me at the time. It still does.

My Own Mental Illness

There was more, though, than just the physical manifestation of grief. The side I tried to keep hidden was the emotional grief I was barely enduring. While putting on a "game face" for the rest of the world, and trying to be there as much as possible for Justin and Conner in their grief, I felt completely isolated and alone. Not eating, not sleeping except with the aid of sleeping pills, feeling trapped in my job, I was truly the walking, breathing dead.

I had no interest in life, except as a façade. With every piece of my own being, I desperately wanted to go to be with Eric. I felt torn between being there for the two sons still living, and wanting to simply give up and die myself, and join Eric, either in nothingness or on the promised other side. I had no preference between those options. I just didn't want to be here any longer.

In early December, trying to maintain some kind of Christmas normalcy for our family, I purchased tickets to the Jimmy Rankin Christmas show in Airdrie, about a half hour north of Calgary and about an hour east of Strathmore. Jimmy was the youngest sibling of the well-known Rankin Family of East Coast musical fame. The day of the event, every single member of the family bailed. However, our dear friends Tracey, her husband Kevin and her mom did join us, along with Kathryn and her parents, David and Margaret. It was an enjoyable evening, despite the frigid winter temperatures we were experiencing, thanks to the deep freeze we were in. With the wind chill, the temperature was near -40 that night.

When it was time to leave, Tracey insisted on driving home with me. At the best of times, I am an introvert. Given the stress I was under, it took everything I had to be part of a social event. I simply wanted to be alone. We argued and negotiated and finally arrived at a compromise. I agreed to text her both when I left and when I arrived safely home.

When the 11:30 p.m. text was sent, Tracey immediately replied that she wasn't going to lie and that she had talked to David about her concerns about me. Suicidal thinking among survivors is very common. I felt frustrated and angry, and sent Margaret a quick text to let her know that Tracey was worried for nothing, that I was simply "appropriately sad."

"Appropriately sad" was my current mantra to explain this emotional state I was in. I was worried about David, as he carried so much survivor guilt, as Eric's doctor and as Kathryn's father. I didn't want him to have the additional concern about me impeding his grief journey. I was frustrated and angry with Tracey for drawing him in.

Within the next few days, the familiar pressure and pain from the ongoing sinus infection was back. I couldn't seem to get on top of it, despite the increasing strength of different antibiotics we were trying. I messaged David's office to see if he could fax a prescription for an antibiotic to the pharmacy. His assistant said he wanted to see me. I assumed it was because they were leaving on holidays and he wanted to be certain we had the infection under control before they left.

When I got there, he wanted to talk to me instead about my depression. Depression? I denied vehemently anything was wrong, or that I was having difficulty coping. After all, I'd always been the one who held everything together for everyone. It was unthinkable, despite all the outward signs to the contrary, that I was anything but in full control of my grief. I was, I reiterated, "appropriately sad."

Tracey had worked for David in the clinic for several years, and he gently reminded me that she had done exactly the right thing in expressing these concerns both to him and I. And I thought that had settled it, from an external observer's position. Internally, I was still barely holding it together. My will to live was a daily choice that I had to make each morning, and again several times during the day.

As we each navigated our grief journey independently, we often didn't speak of what our own struggles were. The experience was completely consuming, and we simply didn't have the energy to be there for anyone else. It was some time later when Justin and I shared the truth with each other—that we had each been deeply suicidal ourselves in the months since Eric's death, but it wasn't something we had given voice to. Conner, months later, admitted to the same struggle.

It was only in hindsight that we were able to take it out and examine it. Wading through the midst of it, we couldn't even recognize it for what it was. Sometimes I wonder if that is what it was like for Eric, during his times of deepest depression. Did he simply not want to bother anyone, believing he could carry it on his own?

The friend whose house I had stayed at on Eric's birthday, Darcy, worked days on and off in Australia. He was home for Christmas, and he came over to the house to catch up. I remember being curled up in the biggest chair in the living room, my head on the arm of it, barely able to even carry on a conversation, so broken was my heart. I talked to him candidly about the darkness I was trapped in. And I questioned why I had resented Tracey's genuine and justified concern. It was as though I was angry at having my façade revealed for being just that.

Darcy was very thoughtful and perceptive, one of the most intelligent people I'd known in my lifetime. He talked about when he was driving a lot for work and was exhausted.

Right thinking would say you should pull over and rest, he explained, especially because he enforced safety as a supervisor. But distorted thinking made you believe you should just push through it and rest when you got home. That analogy still resonates with me as the best way to describe the peripheral awareness of my own depression, but lack of insight as to how bad it was or what to do left me to stumble blindly forward.

Christmas: Another First

And so, Christmas loomed. We were a family that loved to celebrate together. We had long since given up on the meaning of Christmas being tied to any kind of material gifts, although we did our share of consumerism during the holiday season. Our celebrations were always focused on being together and the gift of our deep love for each other. It was Eric's favourite time of the year.

When he was around seven or eight years old, and he first heard the rumblings about what the truth might be about Santa Claus, Eric tested the waters first with Justin. Lying beside his big brother in bed, he asked him, "Tell me the truth, Just, I'm old enough for this. Is it true there isn't a Santa?"

And Justin gave Eric the explanation he himself had heard as a small boy.

"No," Eric screamed in horror, "I said, 'tell me the truth!'"

He then came to me and the scenario pretty much played out all over again. And, from that that day forward, for an entire year, Eric pretended those two conversations had never happened and planned for Christmas as he always had.

After his year of denial, Eric finally accepted what his older brother and I had shared with him. But there was still Conner, two and a half years younger. Eric and I had huddled and discussed that this might be the last year Conner believed in Santa, so it was important it be a very special Christmas. Eric had his elf hat on and was happily decorating the tree when Conner came into the kitchen to talk to me.

"Mom, I know about Santa," he said matter-of-factly. Then he looked over into the living room and whispered to me, "But I'm really starting to worry about Eric."

That was Christmas in our household. Always trying to make it special for each other. The Christmas of 2013 was one none of us knew how to prepare for. So, we didn't. Like Eric, we ignored the reality that was too big to comprehend.

However, I did manage to put up the tree. We also had a family tradition established when Justin was small. We would spend a day doing Christmas baking, box the goodies up and think about who had been a blessing to us in the past year and then deliver the cookies as gifts from the heart. The Christmas of 2013, I didn't think I had it in me to do my annual baking bonanza. But Conner asked me if that was one tradition we could maintain, and so I spent one weekend with our neighbour girl, Jaiden, who had been helping bake since we all moved into the new neighbourhood together. Other than those two small efforts, our labours were centered on having this once-joyous occasion pass as quickly and as painlessly as possible. Justin thought he would be working Christmas Day and wanted it that way. Conner was planning on going with his father somewhere, and I was just going to attend church.

My cousin called me on the 23rd of December. He and his wife were going through town and planned to stop in to visit. I hurriedly went out and bought a turkey and all the fixings for an impromptu Christmas dinner. As it turned out, Justin was on days off and Conner and his father's plans fell through, and so I decided we would have our dinner that day. I invited Tracey and Kevin, as was our custom—to share big family gatherings, particularly Sunday dinners, amongst the neighbours. Ironically, my cousin, whose visit had been the impetus for the turkey dinner, ended up cancelling, but our family and close friends had been drawn together for a traditional dinner. The meal was on the table, and I was still standing near the kitchen island as we said grace. I added one small prayer to the usual blessing.

"Please, God, take care of my angel in Heaven."

As I sat down at the head of the dining room table to join the rest of the family, the chandelier above the table turned off and then on. This was the only time this has ever happened. We all looked up and then at each other but didn't say a word.

Merry Christmas in Heaven, my Eric.

Christmas Eve was exceptionally heavy. It was at 2:20 p.m. that Conner and I looked at each other and decided that we should do something for Christmas. So, we jumped in the car and headed to Cross Iron Mills Mall just north of Calgary, which we anticipated would be pretty empty the afternoon of Christmas Eve.

As we drove, we were surprised by a call from our old neighbour, Jeff, and his partner, Rae, asking whether we were around and whether we would like to join them and their families for Christmas dinner. Having no plans, we took him up on the offer. We managed to get through Christmas Eve by going to a fondue at

Tracey and Kevin's, having Christmas Dinner at our old friends', and me going to Christmas Day mass. I learned that we would dread these days, but we would survive them. Somehow.

7

Seeking Safe Harbour

"'God,' I ask, 'What do I do?' 'You're nothing but a fighter, he replies.'"
—Eric Schmit

Home is Where Our Hearts Are

Most of my family had stayed in Kenaston, and so wherever our paths took us, this really was always home. When the boys were young, it was easy to go back to visit, but as they grew older and were active in their sports and their lives, and mine grew busier as well, the trips became fewer, further between and shorter.

Home in Saskatchewan was a place Eric cherished, despite the passing of years and the shortening of visits. The day he left for Saskatchewan, the weekend that he passed, when he had asked me to go with him and I declined, he remarked that I needed to spend more time there, that everyone loved me so much. In his death, with his final resting spot at the cemetery in Kenaston, he became my impetus to spend more time there.

What I was finding in my grief and loss was a strong connection back to my roots, to the family and community I had neglected for so long in the busyness of my life. This was what Eric had encouraged me to come back and find.

I don't recall exactly which day we headed to Saskatchewan after Christmas, but Conner and I went. Conner found it extremely hard to be back on the farm where he had slept and was awakened to the news about his brother. But he loved his grandmother dearly, and so every time he visited, he would stay for a few minutes and then leave to visit one or the other of his many cousins. But, if he came back to the farm late at night, instead of sleeping in the second spare room, he now crawled into bed beside me.

We spent a few days in Kenaston and for whatever reason I drove back alone. As always, on the long trip I asked Eric for a sign and then whiled away the hours watching and hoping. Shortly after crossing the border into Alberta, I received a Facebook message from another old neighbour. We had left that house in the summer of 2006, but apparently, there was some mail there for us— something that hadn't happened in years.

Upon reading the message, my heart started racing. I didn't think that I could go there. That was really the home the boys had grown up in, eight years of their childhood spent there, and the thought of having to face it was overwhelming. I struggled the entire drive to

Strathmore with whether I could actually go there. And, I wondered, what important mail could possibly be there when it had been so long since we had moved?

It was late and dark, and I was tired. I had decided that no, I wouldn't go get the mail. But, as I got closer to Strathmore, I knew I would be just blocks away when I stopped to check the mail for Darcy, once again in Australia. I resolved to face my fears.

Making the right hand turn down the old familiar street, my stomach was in knots. But imagine my surprise when I pulled up in front of the house and saw the size of the cherry tree the boys and I had planted in the front yard when they were little. I had completely forgotten about it.

As I waited in the landing for the new owners to get the mail, which turned out to be a Christmas card from another family who had lost their son, I asked how they enjoyed the house.

"We love it," the husband said, "especially the cherry tree. You should have seen it in full bloom this spring, and we got 22 pounds of cherries. My wife made pies and jam . . . "

As I left, I took a long look at the cherry tree, barren in winter, silhouetted by the streetlight and the light from the bay window of the house.

Thank you, Eric, for my sign.

Shifting Priorities

As follow-up to meeting him in Ottawa, I had been invited to one of Robb Nash's shows in Calgary. There, I had time to truly reflect and to take in the impact of how Robb's message resonated with the youth. He stayed to speak with every young person who wanted to connect with him personally, and it was really in the last minutes where the magic revealed itself, as those students most in need of conversation and support had waited right until the end. As planned, Robb's team had worked with the schools beforehand to deal with disclosure and providing appropriate supports. He acted as the catalyst for young people to reach out following his show.

There was one message Robb shared that stood out in the two shows. He talked about what he did—a musician who played a guitar, sang and shared his own story. But then he talked about the "Why?" As in, why do we do what we do?

As Christmas passed, I was struggling to find a "Why?" in my work. Along with the stress caused by my grief, there had been transition in the organization, forcing me into a new position; the change tapping the few reserves I had at my disposal.

Although many would advise against a job change in the year following such a tragedy, I happened to hear of a new one in a local mental health organization, in a communications leadership role. Not only was it in the same building where I worked, but, as luck would have it, the former executive director of the agency now worked with me. She suggested that taking my resume in person, in parallel with the online application process, and asking to speak even briefly to the new Executive Director would likely be a wise approach. I followed her lead and fortunately was granted an informal interview the morning of January 31.

Had I not seen Robb's show, I would have presented myself the conventional way the following morning, believing that would be the key to getting an interview and hopefully the job. Instead, as I sat with the executive director in this conversation-style meeting, I spoke of my "why". I shared Eric's story, my own story, and why I wanted the opportunity to bring my unique skills in communications to this position and the important issue of mental health.

The short conversation we had initially planned for morphed into an hour and a half. She remarked about how she had been just reading a book called *Joy Inc.* and how she had been reflecting on how to bring more joy into the workplace. As I left, I told her I had always thought of my name as a responsibility.

I was offered the job shortly after the interview. Throwing conventional wisdom to the wind, I took the leap to make the change, deciding that, if it proved to be a wrong decision, I could start looking again.

The Frozen, Barren Soul

Although Catholic, I'd also never been one to shy away from exploring psychic and other phenomena long condemned by the church. In fact, mere weeks before Eric had passed, one psychic named Patricia Monna had cautioned me that, "As a soul, he doesn't want to be here," and told me we would lose him, to his own hand, before his 21st birthday if he didn't stop drinking.

It wasn't a message I wanted to hear, and so I ignored it. However, when Eric did die, I immediately reached out to her via Facebook and begged her to let me know he was okay. She told me that there was a rule of thumb to let souls who passed have some time to adjust and therefore to wait at least six months. As hard as it was to hear this message, I honoured what she had told me.

There was another clairvoyant medium, also well-known in the Calgary area as Clairvoyant Kim. She has a seven- to nine-month waiting list. That timing fit, and Conner had asked me to book an appointment with her, based on her reputation. So I booked gift readings for Justin and Conner. For some reason, after that first outreach to Patricia, I couldn't bring myself to see a medium. Sadly, I understood the saying that sometimes the heart needed more time to accept what the mind already knew.

Conner was the first to see the renowned medium, and then Justin, both in February. The contents of their readings were private, but there was a single message they brought from Eric meant especially for me: "Please let Mom know I'm okay, and I've found the peace here that I wasn't able to on Earth."

The Present Through the Eyes of the Past

I took the last week of March off between jobs and visited my close friends and former in-laws Val and Randy in Scottsdale, Arizona at their winter home. My relationship with Val had been one of the most precious in my life. Their acreage was incredibly peaceful. I found something about the sun deeply spiritually soothing and so when visiting there, I rose early to watch the sunrise, taking my morning coffee and climbing to the rooftop of the pueblo-style house to enjoy the quiet morning alone. I said a rosary to start the day while watching the shifting colours and listening to the sounds of the desert as it came alive.

My life even prior to Eric's death had been one of constantly chasing deadlines and extreme busyness. In his passing, keeping busy was my survival technique. What I did find in visiting these two who meant so much to me was that their desert home proved to be the one place where I really could unwind. I read, I slept a lot and I found restoration of sorts for my aching heart.

This visit, however, did have another purpose, all part of my quest for understanding the meaning of life and in particular this experience of excruciating pain and loss. I had been reading about Dr. Michael Newton's work in past life regressions and the journey of souls. Following up on discoveries he had made in his clinical practice, Dr. Newton had begun to explore the concept of the afterlife through the eyes of his clients, using hypnotherapy. As a result of his research, he wrote several books and founded The Newton Institute, where it was possible to receive training to help individuals access memories stored in the subconscious through deep hypnosis.

Val had been interested in the area for years and we had many conversations around it, even prior to Eric's death. Now my interest was more than mere curiosity. I needed to consider the validity of this particular concept relative to life's meaning. I searched online for therapists who had been trained at The Newton Institute and found several in the Phoenix area. I connected with a few through emails and phone conversations and decided to have a past life regression while on my holiday. After interviewing multiple therapists, there was one who stood out, Robin Davison. I had a sense that seeing her was far more than a simple business transaction and that her heart was genuinely focused on the helpfulness of the journey and what she could do to facilitate that.

The idea of a past life regression is that tapping into these memories in the subconscious allows you to see your soul's experiences in other bodies, and in doing so, to achieve a higher awareness and understanding of your soul and the experiences you had while living. The purpose could be to help understand a current life experience, such as abuse or addiction, or a seemingly irrational fear, and could also be helpful in dealing with grief. I'd never thought about the concept of multiple lives, other than peripherally, before. But in my new search for meaning, I wondered whether I might find answers for my own life and the many twists and turns it had had, and mostly this latest journey of tragedy and unimaginable loss.

The morning of the regression, Val and I drove together to Phoenix. I really had no idea what to expect.

As Robin helped me enter a hypnotic state, I was surprised at my awareness of everything around me. We went through a few processes and then she asked me to go to a life where there was something I needed to know. As I entered this lifetime, I reported back to her that I was standing on a hillside. There was a small, white church in front of me. It had low walls and a rounded face that extended higher than the roof, and there was the smell of a wood fire burning somewhere behind me. She asked me how I felt, and I replied that I was calm. There was nothing ominous about the fire. It was like experiencing a moment in time.

She asked me what I was wearing, and I described in detail the black shoes, the dress with the white apron around it. I told her I was 15 years old, and that the time was somewhere in the 1700s. The answers leapt from me, without any sense of where they were coming from.

I then ran down the hill. The grass was green, but dry, and there were small white stones all over the hillside. I approached a small house. It was made of stone, with a low doorway and single window to the left of the entry. The roof was thatched.

As I came down the hill, my father came through the stooped doorway. He was wearing typical peasant attire: a white shirt, vest, black pants and a hat. We didn't talk; he simply hugged me in his big bear hug. I was so excited when I recognized him as my father in this lifetime. In the massive hug, I felt immense unconditional love. He took me inside the house and I sat at the table, directly in front of the door, an interior wall with a doorway was to the right of it. The table was made of rough-hewn timber, but what I remember the most was that there weren't chairs. Rather, what he sat me down on was a tree stump, which served as a chair.

That piece of my regression behind me, she asked me to go to the next place in this lifetime that I needed to learn from. I had just given birth to a little boy. The room was large, the bed big and the frame made of timber as well. It was murky, with the darkness of wood everywhere, a larger door to the left of the head of the bed, and what little light coming in was streaming through a skylight, bound by the same log-style structure that was common throughout my experience. She asked if there was anyone there I knew, and I said there were many people standing at the foot of the bed, and the only one

I recognized was my brother Dallas from this life. He was standing with his hat in hand and was very solemn, but proud of this baby. She asked if the baby's father was there and I said that he wasn't. As I looked at the baby boy, I recognized him as Justin, my oldest son in this life. I felt complete and filled with love.

Neither of these experiences seemed to shed any light on what I was experiencing in this life. In hindsight, I believe the greatest message for me was that of unconditional love. Over the years, I'd lost the ability to have compassion for myself, and even more so to love myself. It has been a long time since I had simply felt the love that came without any strings attached, yet I experienced it in both moments I remembered.

She asked me to go where I needed to next in this lifetime. I was standing and looking up at a wall of stone and bushes with clouds behind. A cherubic, blonde, curly-haired angel reached out and pulled me in. I told her I thought I was in Heaven, and then I recognized the angel as Eric. My heart leapt with joy. I had missed him so!

He was dressed in a white robe, with a braided gold rope sash around the waist. And he had wings. He told me that he was my guide, and he showed me a big book with a feather pen laying between the pages. This, he explained, was the contract our souls had agreed to before coming to Earth in this life. Eric asked me to tell our story. We sat on some rocks in this garden, facing each other, our heads together and my hands in his. He told me how he loved me and was always with me.

Robin then asked another guide to come in. I recognized him as my friend and brother-in-law Gary, Eric's paternal uncle who had also died by suicide at 22 years of age, long before he could meet any of my children. He was wearing a tan–coloured burlap robe. He stood at a small distance and while no words were spoken, I understood that he was Eric's guide and counsel, teaching him, quietly, gently, wisely, guiding the process.

Then Eric took me, and from a place somewhere above, he showed me the world. He told me this was my path and I needed to go and follow this path, but to take my time. He showed me a tiny, beautiful seaside village, with old buildings and orange rooftops, and told me it was there I needed to go to write, that I would be at peace there. I asked him what the message was, and he said it was about love, and hope.

From there, we went to a balcony. It was white stone with pillars. We looked down upon a grey dark stone building, with a stone floor where I saw men in shackles. I could feel their emotional pain as well as the darkness, dampness and cold. Although they were in shackles, they weren't bound to this stone floor. Their eyes were downcast. Then one looked up towards me, a light shone in and a chasm formed between this man and the others. The more the light shone, the larger the crack appeared and soon this man was bathed in colour. Eric explained to me that this was the story of addiction, and that I need to shine the light by bringing a message of hope in my writings. "Be the light Mom. You are the light," he said.

As we stood together, Eric asked me to let go of guilt, of not feeling good enough, of feeling like a failure, and of having given up; he told me that these no longer served me. He said he had brought me much help and he would continue bringing it to me, that he cleared the path ahead. And then he showed me the world one more time and simply said, "It is time, but take your time, Mom."

I can't say I came out with the clarity, or comfort, I had hoped to find. If anything, I was somewhat confused; had this really happened or was it simply my imagination, the conjectures of a mother so overcome with grief she needed to create something?

On our way back to the acreage, Val and I talked about our experiences, and the only thing that really stood out was that when I described how Gary, her brother, had appeared, she told me that this was the same way he had appeared in her previous regression. Outside of that, the experience left me with more questions than answers. And, despite Eric's confidence in my journey, I wasn't certain that my path would be so easy to follow. More importantly, for weeks after the regression, I longed to go back to that space I had shared with Eric, where I felt absolute love and freedom from the weight of this world with its sadness and loss.

Connecting Through Song

The next time I made the trip home to Kenaston was for Easter. The morning I was heading back to Calgary, I stopped at the cemetery as always. As I stood at Eric and Dad's gravesite, I threw my hands up in the air and screamed at the sky in agony, "Why the fuck can't I just talk to him, God? Why?" as tears poured down my face.

The instant I cried out, my cell phone went off in the pocket of my winter coat. At first, I thought perhaps it was someone calling, although it was blaring loud and I didn't have ring tones attached to callers. It was an iTunes song, playing so loudly it completely startled me. I had never used iTunes on my phone. I'd never downloaded a single song. And yet, as clear as day, the lyrics to a genre I had never listened to and a song I had never heard before were playing. The first words I understood left me dumbfounded. The first line, "When you're near me/I'm yelling and you can't hear me," followed by sentiments about wasted days and not being able to face them and all that we were. The final line said we were living in a heartbreak dream.

The song was called *Heartbreak Dream* by Betty Who. I stood there, phone in hand, staring at the sky. Could it really be an answer to my anguished cry? I collected myself and went back to the car and tried to download the song.

As I sat in my car outside of the cemetery gate, my cousins came up, on their way to visit their mother's gravesite. I rolled down the window to the car and told them about my experience. I couldn't get the song to download again, but I did save it on my phone so that I could listen to it when I returned home. This experience of music downloading itself and randomly playing never happened again.

Later that week, I was having lunch with one of the other managers from my previous job, a good friend. Now into full-blown determination to solve the mystery of life and death, I shared with her that I had also booked a reading with the medium Justin and Conner had gone to. I told her it would be months before I would get to go. Generous by nature, she told me she also had a reading booked, but it was the next day. She wanted to switch readings with me. She said that she was just going for interest and so it didn't make a difference to her as to the timing of her reading. She could see how desperate I was to find a connection to my son.

I accepted with trepidation. As much as I appreciated what I interpreted as these ongoing messages, and clear connections to Eric, I was somehow worried. What if nothing came through? This would mean that life ended with our physical existence. If there was nowhere to find my son in the afterlife, then how would I go on? I was hopeful, excited, anxious and scared all at once. But I accepted her generous offer to go see this renowned medium.

My father was first through to speak to me. As much as I loved my father, and still do, as awful as it sounds, my heart sank for a moment. It was Eric I so desperately needed to hear from, to find comfort and confirmation in the afterlife.

The next message was that a young man was there. That he and his Grandpa were always there. There were multiple messages of comfort.

He talked about being happy, about being with us all the time, in our vehicles. He told me we were never alone. Then she said something that didn't make sense to her—something about enjoying watching Justin sweat. I explained to her that as I was having my reading, Justin was in the process of cutting weight for his upcoming fight that Friday night. As part of this, he would be sweating out 10 to 20 pounds in the infrared sauna to make his weight class. It was a tortuous process, and as they did this many times together preparing for fights, I have no doubt Eric would have enjoyed immensely watching Justin go through it!

She talked about how he visited his grandma every afternoon as she had her tea and toast. And said that as she sat and drank her tea, she looked at Eric's picture. Eric had a close relationship with his grandmother Carmella. We would always laugh about how he was such a "Grandma's boy". This was the grandmother he had stayed with the summer before he died, the grandmother who found him.

Then she mentioned the cemetery. She identified, and I confirmed, that he rested in a cemetery where I visited him. Then she said there was something about the cemetery and music he was trying to explain. His message was to not question that it was him, that indeed he had been with me. I told her the story about the song on my iPhone.

As in the readings for his brothers, Eric also told me that he had found what had been elusive for him in this life, happiness. That he had battled depression for so long and was simply exhausted and unable to go on. But he said that I was a wonderful mom, and not to doubt that at all.

He talked about the complicated relationship the boys had with their father and how the other two had handled it differently, and that the good that would come out of his death would be their father spending more time with his brothers now. Then Eric told me to give Conner a big hug; he was trying to be so brave and was hiding his pain. But not to worry, he would be okay.

He talked about his birthday party and the chocolate cupcakes Kathryn had made for him, describing them right down to the blue icing.

I asked about what he wanted his headstone to be like. She described a picture of him playing hockey where he was looking up and the stick was down, and said that was what he wanted, from when he was enjoying his life.

He had also shown her the cherry tree in front of her own house and explained how it had been a gift to her from a family who had also lost their son to suicide. I shared with her my dream about Eric and the cherry tree blossoms, and how when I saw images of cherry tree blossoms, I counted it as a message, an undeniable symbol of connection and love.

As we wrapped up the reading, she said Eric wanted me to know that he was on holidays with me and that I would be going on another holiday soon, a beautiful island holiday. And he told me that I would know when it would be time to write his story, not to rush to do it. Finally, he thanked me for his strong Viking name, and then the reading was over.

I seemed to be lulled into a new pattern of complacency in my grief, one of endurance. Naively, I would later learn, I assumed I had reached the stage in my grief journey of "acceptance." I was so far from accepting anything. I was simply numb, still the walking, breathing dead.

The Painful Surprises

There had been some monumental obstacles to overcome in the days, weeks and months following Eric's death. His birthday had been difficult, but we had steeled ourselves for that experience. Likewise, Christmas had been predictably difficult, but we had prepared and walked through it as best we could. May would bring another difficult day, but this time not one I had anticipated.

As Mother's Day loomed, I had an early alarm bell go off internally, that perhaps this might be a hard day, but I rationalized that I was still a mother and nothing, not even Eric's death, could change that. However, the week leading up to Mother's Day not only caught me by surprise but completely sidelined me.

The Thursday prior to Mother's Day, I could feel myself beginning the now-familiar spiral downward. I got up for work and made it through the day, but as soon as I got in the car to drive home, I broke down. The next day was the same. I cried on the commute, I screamed in my sorrow and I fell into bed to end the day in a grief-induced depressive episode. Saturday morning, I forced myself to go to the gym, and made it through my workout, but as soon as I got into the car, the tears once again began to fall, and I cried all the way home.

Crying, for me, was a double-edged sword. While many found release in it, for me it was a trigger for my already-chronic migraines. As a result, I tried to avoid crying whenever possible and repress the emotion. I was finding it impossible to do in this loss.

There were two days where I learned the origin of the term "broken heart": the day of Eric's funeral and my first Mother's Day without him. On both days, the physical sensation of absolute physical pain in the left side of my chest made me feel like my heart had literally been broken in two. I felt it crack. There was no other way to describe it; it wasn't the bottomless emotion of sadness that comes with grief. It was an actual physical experience.

As I sat sobbing in the driveway after arriving home from the gym, a number I didn't recognize came up on my phone. I generally didn't answer unknown numbers, especially out-of-province. As I was enduring a full-blown emotional breakdown, it was even more unlikely that I would answer. But for whatever reason, I decided to. It was Robb Nash calling, the musician I had met in Ottawa and later seen in Calgary. He said that he couldn't get me off of his mind and really felt compelled to call me.

We talked for a long time as I sat in my car in the driveway. He shared a lot about his music and the meaning behind the lyrics in many of his songs. I told him about my desire to write this book and my desperate search for not only meaning but confidence that there was something more than this human experience we have here on Earth. I found the courage to ask him the question that had been on my mind since first hearing his story—what had he seen during the time he was clinically dead and later clinging to life in the months of his coma? Or was there nothing at all?

Robb gently answered me, as I now know he does to the many others who pose this same question, that he doesn't feel he is supposed to share the experience of what he saw. But he assured me that without a doubt, there was far more to this experience than the here and now.

There is an honesty that comes when your internal resources are completely depleted by tragedy. If there is a gift in experiencing some of life's most painful experiences, it is that you lose pretense of any kind. The conversations that Mother's Day weekend were powerful, and I found some of the strength I needed right in that conversation to survive the awful moments.

Leaving Something Better Behind

The impact of tragedy is overwhelming, and overwhelmingly unique. Each remaining family member, once part of a circle so tight people would comment on it, was now completely fractured in grief. How to realign?

Justin was working in the oil patch as a directional driller. Conner was completing his aviation training. I was holding onto a home base that didn't feel much like a home anymore.

The one thing the three boys had always had in common and had taught me to love as well was physical fitness—it started with a decision to meet them "where they're at". I knew that to spend time with my boys, it had to be doing something they loved, hence our time together at the gym. After Eric's death, it wasn't so much a decision, but survival, that led us to open a mixed martial arts training facility in Strathmore.

The gym, although a family business, was really set up for Justin to run, along with his partner at the time, Lisa. For Justin, it was a big leap from the steady and substantial salary of the oil patch, but in the aftermath of loss offered something to bring our family back together and learn how to function without this big, important piece of the family unit. This gym gave everyone something to throw themselves into, and physical fitness was something we had always used as our connection point.

Justin and Lisa took great care in designing the gym to differentiate it from the others in the community, so it didn't tap into an already over-served market. It was tapping into a brand-new market—mixed martial arts and sports team training with instructor-led programs.

I was always extremely grateful that I had my own boys who had guided me through building a program and then feeling comfortable at the gym. Too often, I observed people buying memberships and genuinely wanting to get their bodies healthy and well, but without the knowledge and support to create a successful environment. And few people could afford personal trainers to help them develop the required regime and commitment. The result was that they ended up quitting. The concept of a gym where members always had someone working with them, advising, motivating and encouraging made so much sense to me at an intuitive level. I remembered fondly how Eric had first motivated me to walk past the intimidation I felt at going to a gym and to start on my own wellness program, and how training with any of the three boys at any given time gave me a feeling of connection to them.

Eric not only loved and lived physical fitness and the time he would share with his brothers training towards one goal or another, but he really understood the importance of fitness and emotional wellness—the inter-connectedness of the mind, body and soul. This was why Eric had taken his Personal Training certification and was pursuing it through college. One of the greatest gifts of that last summer was in watching him work one-on-one with his clients.

When he first started training me, one of the things I remember most was him telling me that I would notice the confidence I would gain. Throughout my teens and adult life, I struggled with confidence. In my mind, self-worth could be found in thinness, and I dieted obsessively to maintain a lithe figure. Despite my lower weight, I wore loose fitting clothes, as though I was embarrassed to have anyone see my body. Over the months that I trained, my confidence was transformed. I was not only gaining weight but building muscle and mass—and I wasn't embarrassed at all by my physique. I was learning to be proud of it—wearing clothing that fit—even though I was bigger than before.

As Eric worked with other clients, I saw him shine in being able to tap into their hidden self-confidence, encouraging and inspiring. This was truly a gift, and one we all intuitively knew, even if we didn't acknowledge it, that we could bring to others, and in doing so have Eric's memory live on.

The gym was also built on an anti-bullying mantra. Although everyone in the family was acutely aware that several factors had led to Eric's final decision to end his life, we all remembered the difficult time he had experienced in junior high and the bullying which had contributed so much to the difficulties he experienced in those years.

The week before his death, a young high school student messaged Eric. He wanted to learn how to fight because he was being bullied. Eric not only invited him over and trained him for a while, he went out and bought him training gear—everything he could need. That was the generosity Eric espoused. He really had no attachment to anything material—if anything he was quite ethereal. He would spend every cent of his pay cheque, most it going towards others, and then borrow from me to get through to the next payday. But, honest to the core, the first thing he would do when his payday came was pay me back whatever I was owed.

Being so generous meant he often went without. But not being attached to labels, Eric was happy to find himself a cheap pair of white, store-brand runners at Walmart. Justin was very much the opposite, image-conscious, so he would be on Eric about the runners.

"If you needed shoes, why didn't you just ask me?"

I remember Eric throwing his gym gear into the truck when he left for the farm that fated weekend for a stop to train before he got on the road. When Justin opened the door to his truck, a single white Walmart runner tumbled to the ground in front of him.

Greeting everyone at APEX MMA (our family business) is a single white and green, Walmart-brand runner, hanging from the cage. It serves as a reminder for those of us who understood the meaning, the reason we are all there—to leave our egos at the door and focus on what it important. In the gym and in life.

One of the many times Justin and I talked about Eric, recognizing that our loss wasn't unique and figuring out how to learn to live again, Justin pointed out to me the impact Eric's death had made because of how we chose to work through it.

"Look at the lives the gym has changed, Mom, the kids who can come here and feel safe. And find belonging. And look at the work you do now. None of this would have happened if he hadn't died. Remember that. Eric was our warrior, a true soldier. He died so that others could live."

The Meaning of Roots

By the time summer hit, the dreaded one-year anniversary was looming. Justin, Conner and I talked at length about what we would do, where we would be, how we would acknowledge it. Some families referred to this as their Angel Birthday. Despite the amount of thought put into it, we really had no idea how we would spend Eric's first Angel Birthday.

In late June, my cousin Lynne Yelich texted me that she had to be in Croatia for meetings in both Dubrovnik and then later in Zagreb, with a span of about 10 days in between. Lynne, whom I'd always had a very special relationship with—more like a sister than a cousin—wasn't going as a simple tourist. At the time, she was the Conservative Member of Parliament for Arm River and Minister of State for Foreign Affairs, giving her responsibilities over things like foreign embassies and issuing passports. While her upcoming trip overseas included official duties, she asked if it would be possible for me to join her and a couple others to travel with her during her non-working days to our shared ancestral village of Lovinac, Croatia. She shared that she had hoped this trip might bring me some peace as I struggled towards the anniversary of losing Eric.

The evening I arrived, we went for supper at a resort owned by a young Croat who had been raised in Canada but whose family had returned to participate in the reconstruction following the wars of the 1990s. We sat on the lovely patio of the restaurant, and enjoyed the sunset view while visiting. A young man just entering the priesthood, Domigoj, with roots in Lovinac, also joined us. He and I were seated together at the end of the table nearest the water. At just 23 years of age, he reminded me so much of my own sons. As we disbanded for the night and all prepared to go our separate ways, he invited Lynne and I to Sunday morning mass in the ancient 13th-century monastery within old Dubrovnik where he was studying.

I slept in the following morning, and by the time I arrived, the church—which served as an historic art gallery as well—was quiet, as mass had already ended, so I had a few moments to look around and take in its beauty. I sat with the two priests there and talked. The younger knew of my story of loss from our conversation the evening before, and his superior, Father Nicola, and I talked about mental illness and family tragedies. The three of us then sat in the front row and recited a rosary together.

Father Nicola asked if he could do some special prayers for me. He and Domigoj led Lynne and I through to the residencies of the monastery and into a second-floor room. Father Nicola placed his hands on my head and prayed deeply and passionately in both English and Croatian. When finished, he sat beside me and held my hands, telling me, as I listened through tear-filled eyes, that I had an important journey ahead of me, that he had asked God to accompany me on it and that today was just the beginning.

As it was now time to leave, the priests walked us to the gates. As we neared the exit, Domigoj said he needed to get something and asked for us to wait. He ran upstairs to his room and came back with a rosary in hand. He explained to me that it was the rosary of the Divine Mercy and that the red and white beads were representative of the blood and water which flowed from Christ's side. The Divine Mercy is based on devotion to the endless merciful love of God towards all people and based on the apparitions of Jesus received by Saint

Faustina Kowalska. Faustina reported many apparitions, visions and conversations with Jesus.

We were leaving Dubrovnik to go to Medjugorje— considered by many Catholics one of the sacred pilgrimage sites in the world—in Bosnia. Bosnia, part of the former Yugoslavia, was politically separate from Croatia, but had a highly-concentrated Croatian and Catholic population. Domigoj explained to me that it was when he was visiting Medjugorje that he had made the decision to enter the priesthood and follow this path towards God. He handed me his precious rosary as a gift for my journey.

The priests walked with us to the edge of the Old City, their white robes flowing, and bade us farewell as we organized our rental car and headed inland towards Medjugorje.

Medjugorje translated means "between mountains". Since 1981, when six local children said they had seen visions of the Blessed Virgin Mary, Medjugorje has become a place of Christian pilgrimage. According to the six young visionaries, the Blessed Mother—or Gospa as she is known in Croatia—had a simple message to share: to tell the world to return to the ways of God, and to convert their lives to peace with God and with their fellow man.

The Catholic Church follows a criterion for evaluating apparitions. There were two possible judgments. They were, in Latin (still the working language at the Vatican): *constat de supernaturalitate* (it is confirmed to be of supernatural origin) and *non constat* (it is not confirmed). The Church had made successive comments that it could not confirm the supernatural nature of the apparitions. A commission set by the Vatican's Congregation for the Doctrine of Faith to study Medjugorje concluded its work in January of 2014, but the results were not released. On June 6, 2015, Pope Francis told reporters, "We've reached the point of making a decision." To date, though, that decision has not been made public and the miraculous claims made about Medjugorje remained *non constat*.

The story of Medjugorje was one I was familiar with, partly because of my Croatian roots, but also because of the deep faith of my mother. Her pedigree was distinctly French-Canadian, and she had been a faithful follower of the Catholic religion her entire life, which included having attended boarding school at a convent, led by the nuns.

Not long before he passed, Eric happened to see a book at my house that he had given his grandmother for her previous birthday, *The Five People You Meet in Heaven*.

"Why is this here," he asked. "Didn't Grandma read it??"

I answered that yes, she had, and had lent it to me the last time I was there.

Then he replied offhandedly, as was Eric's style, "I guess she doesn't need to read a book. She already knows."

This reference was to her own near-death experience when she was six years old. Her appendix had burst, and her heart stopped on the operating table. The doctors, even with their limited medical technology in rural

Saskatchewan in the early 1940s, restarted her heart. When she came back, she spoke of a place of incredible light and indescribably beautiful music. It was this experience to which we often her attributed her unshakeable faith despite the many trials of life. She doesn't often speak of the experience, but in a recent visit she told me that regardless of what she had experienced in her life, nothing could compare the beauty of what she saw and heard in those moments.

Mom had been at a parish book sale and found a book called *Miracle at Medjugorje* by Wayne Weible. Mom was profoundly moved by this book, as it was written by a Lutheran newspaper publisher and columnist who had originally written articles on modern day miracles. He heard of the apparitions in this tiny village and began his own investigative journey. The book was his story of how four Christmas newspaper columns on Medjugorje changed the direction of his life.

Mom had given me the book and I, too, had read it. I had enjoyed it thoroughly, but at the time had no intention of going to Croatia, or Medjugorje, or really held any travel plans. When I had read the book, my life was consumed with completing my Masters' degree and making sure there was going to be enough money to help both Eric and Conner complete their post-secondary education.

Two years after reading the book, and almost a year following Eric's death, there I was, set to visit that sacred village. The trip to Medjugorje was the real reason my cousin had wanted me to come to Croatia. The rest of the journey was about connecting with our familial roots. But this part was important to her, because she knew how deeply I was struggling and was hoping I would find some peace in my loss by reconnecting with our faith.

She and I, and a young woman from Zagreb who served as our interpreter, began the walk up the stony mountainside. Here, at the first stop, she explained to us that this was where the children had fled when the Communists had come to remove them from their families. On the hillside, they reported being kept miraculously safe by the Virgin, who cloaked them in invisibility by hiding the children beneath her robes as Communist soldiers scoured the fields searching for them. The journey started at a large cross in the hillside to reflect this first incident. Then we climbed the stony mountainside, as approximately 30 million other pilgrims had done since 1981, stopping at various Stations of the Cross, a 14-step Catholic devotion that commemorates Jesus Christ's last day on Earth, to reflect.

When we reached the top and started on our way down again, the interpreter asked to take my picture. I initially refused, preferring to be on the other side of the camera. However, she and my cousin convinced me to allow my photo to be taken to mark my visit, saying that you always needed to plan as though you might never get back. She took several pictures, and then we completed our walk down the stone covered hillside.

That night, we stayed at our guide's parents' villa. As we sat and looked at the pictures from the day, we also looked at the ones on my phone. The first four pictures the guide had taken of me were identical. However, the fifth one had a beautiful ray of pink light, which originated in the sky to my right. The band of light widened throughout the photo.

It was my cousin who immediately connected this and said, "Take out your rosary. The light is the same," referring to the picture where light streams from Jesus's side.

Its colour was indeed almost identical to the image of Jesus on the Divine Mercy rosary which Domigoj had given me.

Like each experience before, I did not find an automatic healing or peace. I placed it in the big box of questions I still felt needed to be answered as to where my son was, whether there truly was a Heaven, or whether this earthly journey was simply that and nothing more. No answer, no sign, while obvious to others, seemed to be enough to ease the pain in my grief-stricken mother's heart.

The following day, we travelled to Lovinac, which was the village where our family had originated. Centuries of history resided here, literally on the last frontier, where Christian soldiers stopped advancing Muslim soldier in battles in the 15th and 16th centuries. Here, in what was now this tiny country again, generations upon generations had experienced oppression, war and poverty, until some fortunate souls had been given the opportunity for a kinder, gentler life in the prairies of Canada—my grandparents among them.

Zeljka, the young priest's mother, but also the doctor's wife in this little village, had connected to Lynne several years ago. She acted as our translator and guide. The rocky hillside, the green grass, the ancient architecture and stone not only told the story of a scenic remote village, but also graphically showed the destruction of war. Here we saw abandoned villages, with empty homes that revealed the magnitude of the war. Whether centuries old stone, or more modern structures, roofs were destroyed, buildings were burned, and even if some were still inhabited at times there were mortar shell attacks evident in the remaining walls. Churches especially dotted the landscape as abandoned buildings with only the stone still intact, the only parts to have survived the fires which were lit as part of the demolition.

We were quiet as we drove through the villages that had, prior to this, only been locations on a map, or names attached to stories from our childhood: Gospic, Lika, Svete Rok, and finally Lovinac.

One of our first places to visit was the cemetery in Lovinac. This was where my great-grandparents, and great aunts and uncles were resting. It was serene and beautifully kept. I later learned that during the war, the graveyard had been desecrated. The first casualties in the destruction when the Serbian soldiers entered a village were churches, hospitals and cemeteries. As a Croatian stronghold, Lovinac was subjected to widespread destruction. Very little of the old cemetery remained as the soldiers went through. Despite the poverty of the area, these were rebuilt to lovingly honour the ancestors in the post-war construction phase.

The roads throughout the area were really trails, which seemed not to have a geographic pattern to them. Some split left, some split right. East, west, north and south didn't seem to have been considered when the farms were built.

As we came to the end of one of these trails, we saw a tiny farm nestled below a big rock which jutted out of the wall face, Budoc Rok, a few kilometres out of Lovinac. The pretty white house, the old stone barn behind, the simple gardens and fruit trees, were a picturesque draw as we made our entry into the long driveway. As we stopped the car and got out, we were greeted from the front step by a woman who appeared to be in her mid-seventies.

She warmly welcomed us into her home. Once again, I was taken by how much of the former culture of this area had been reflected in my own upbringing; I felt as though I was in my grandmother's house. Even its physical appearance reminded me of the home on the family farm in Kenaston. Religious photos adorned the wall. She brought out biscuits and juice, and we were offered a meal.

As she and Zeljka, the doctor's wife, went through the conversation that would lead to understanding about who we were and the purpose of our visit, Zeljka looked at me and smiled. Our accidental stop at this quaint little farm was one that had brought me to my own family. This was the farm my grandfather had been born on. Tears welled in the old woman's eyes as she held my hands and said in Croatian, "Your blood has brought you home."

We had a short visit and went outside to the barn. Here stood the one wall of the old house, reduced to rubble in the war. The one salvageable wall had now been incorporated into the newer structure. She showed us how the house had faced towards the village, and I could see where the door and window once were. I asked if I could take some stones, and gathered some for my two brothers, for Justin and Conner, and for myself.

The visit to Lovinac was profound in many ways. I had never visited Croatia or the home of my grandparents before. Yet, interestingly, each place I visited was distinctly familiar. I had seen it or something markedly similar during the past life regression mere months before. At the time, I had been confused by the experience and didn't talk about it. I worried more that speaking of it would lead others to question my sanity—had my grief indeed caused me to lose my mind?

Here, in the little village set on stony soil, amidst centuries of history and culture, these memories came flooding back. The little white church at the top of the hill where I had been standing, the old stone house with furniture carved from roughhewn wood, the style of the building, from the roof to the door and window frame, the dry grassy landscape that somehow managed to exist in the rocky soil, the white rocks, they were one thing. But even the peasant style of dress from the memories in the regression were reflected in pictures I now saw as we visited family. And later, as we visited the UNESCO World Heritage Sites of Split and Trogir, I could see on the outskirts a similarity in the tiny fishing villages to the one Eric had shown me, where he said I was to go to write.

The days in Croatia held many moments which impacted me profoundly, and somehow served to tie together the meaning I couldn't initially derive from the past life regression months earlier.

And then I was home again. Home from Croatia. Home from home. I felt somewhat grounded as I now faced this dreaded first year anniversary of losing Eric.

I had not yet integrated any of the experiences into anything more than just days. I was still trying to understand my emotions, the overwhelming grief that could strike in any moment and drive me to my knees. The psychics I had seen, the past life regression, the churches in Croatia, the hillside of Medjugorje, each and every day as I continued to process this new life were like another piece of a scattered puzzle that I hadn't even begun to try to assemble. Rather, they were in a box that I hadn't yet opened, and it seemed they were continuously being shaken.

The Dreaded First, Worst Anniversary

And so the first anniversary was finally upon us. How to acknowledge this awful day? It certainly wasn't like his birthday where, although we could measure our loss, we could also remember the gift that had been given in the life Eric had shared and brought to us. Not so much August 4, the August long weekend in Alberta. This day represented the single worst day of all our lives—when the "before" changed to the "after." It was two days— the Sunday morning of the August long weekend, and then the actual date of August 4. The timing of his death meant we would forever be left with two difficult days each year that represented his passing.

We felt compelled somehow to mark the anniversary, and in the end, it was our need to be together that kept us at home in Strathmore.

I was sitting with some friends on my deck when Justin and Conner came barreling into the house in full Mexican luchador wrestling regalia. This included colourful masks and trunks, accessorized with flowing capes. They'd decided to run with the bulls at the Strathmore Heritage Days Rodeo in honour of their brother.

The Strathmore version of the annual run was into its 11th year and didn't have a lot in common with what one might think of its origins in Pamplona, Spain. The resemblance ended with the fact that there were bulls and people running. Costumes increased the visual value, and injuries were not unheard of. It was more circus-like than reminiscent of either a western rodeo or the centuries-old European version. But it drew fans and was a highlight of the event.

Interestingly, that day I didn't have the usual maternal fear that accompanied me when I knew they were about to do something dangerous, or foolish, or both. A mother who had also lost a son shared this with me: "You will never worry again." Check. True story.

While this maternal fear should have kicked into high gear, given the outrageousness of what they were about to do, I was strangely calm. In that moment, it was almost as though I had an acceptance that life will bring what it will. Regardless of how much we fear, prepare, worry, what will be will be—even for my two bad-enough-to-be-interesting sons trying to mark the awful anniversary in their own way. Although there were a few injuries, Justin and Conner thankfully weren't amongst them. They bonded through their laughter. And the uniqueness of their costumes and very fit, tattooed bodies made for great media coverage. They were featured in multiple stories on the weekend news.

Myself, I went to bed early and rose for church. While I typically went to Mary Mother of the Redeemer for mass, for the anniversary I instead met Kathryn and her mother Margaret at St. Mary's Cathedral in downtown Calgary.

On Kathryn's birthday, short weeks after Eric had died, we had gone to St. Mary's and then across the street to a convent belonging to the order of the Faithful Companions of Jesus, where the quiet gardens featured a meditation area and a walking labyrinth, and where I had purchased Eric's rosary. Labyrinth walking is an ancient practice used by many different faiths for spiritual centering, contemplation and prayer. Entering the path of a labyrinth, the walker would walk slowly while quieting their mind and focusing on a spiritual question or prayer. Unlike a maze, the labyrinth has one path to the centre and then back out. This symbolized a journey to a predetermined destination, such as a pilgrimage to a holy site, or the journey through life. On Kathryn's birthday, the three of us had walked through the gardens and meditated in the peaceful summer afternoon at the labyrinth, stopping to pray at a small grotto dedicated to the Blessed Mother.

On this, the first anniversary of Eric's death, we went back. This time, however, we went to mass. We stood together at the back of the cathedral. Kathryn brought the rosary I had given her after Eric died, and I was holding my own when the priest came up and asked if we would take the gifts up.

It was an honour to be asked and typically, when the gifts were presented, you bowed and then made your way back to your seats. However, this time the priest stopped us and asked to do a prayer. The opportunity to present the gifts and then the additional blessing brought me a sense of being very close to my son, as his faith had been so very strong. At this juncture, mine, by contrast, was so very weak. Fragile though it was, it was all I had to cling to.

Following mass, we went for lunch and then went our separate ways. I was so moved by the priest and his blessings that I found the church's email account and sent a message of gratitude, expressing why we had gone and what the service had meant to us, particularly the opportunity to present the gifts and to receive this special blessing. A few days later, I received the loveliest reply from the priest:

> *Your gracious and kind e-mail was passed on to me. I must say that your presence and presentation of the gifts was a source of joy and blessing for me. Thank you for sharing the reason for your presence. I want to share with you a very moving and comforting reflection by Fr. Karl Rahner—a reflection on the reality of our communion with the saints.*
>
> *"The great and sad mistake of many people is to imagine that those whom death has taken leave us. They do not leave us. They remain! Where are they? In darkness? Oh, no! It is we who are in darkness. We do not see them, but they see us. Their eyes, radiant with glory, are fixed upon us. Oh, infinite consolation!*

Though invisible to us, our dead are not absent. They are living near us, transfigured ... into light, into power, into love."

In reflection, we all found our way through the one-year anniversary in the way that made the most sense to us. The odds of me running with the bulls, or even being at a rodeo, were pretty remote, yet I know Eric in Heaven would have been running alongside his brothers. I also believe he was standing with Kathryn, Margaret and I in that lovely old church where we had once sought refuge in the earliest days of our grief.

The first anniversary of Eric's death had passed and while we had dreaded its arrival, upon its departure it was evident this was just to be another day living with the loss of our loved one. As expressed by others who had gone before us, the anticipation of those event days proved to be more difficult than the day itself. Whether his birthday, Christmas or this anniversary, this certainly proved to be the case. The days came and went, and our grief remained.

Chasing, Chasing, Chasing

Within the week after the anniversary, I made an appointment to see a new psychic medium, Debby Fleming. I consciously decided to not disclose anything—recognizing that in all the previous messages, I had either confessed the loss of my son, or the reading or message came from someone who knew us and the story. As much as I appreciated those messages, I was always left with an element of doubt.

It seemed so hard to wrap my head around. I still hadn't truly accepted that he was gone. And if indeed he had gone, I didn't have a clear idea of where. It reflected the messy state of my own faith, and as a result, I had this desperate need to find absolute irrefutable proof that life continued beyond death.

As I booked the reading, I gave nothing away. When the day of the reading arrived, I sat in the driveway of her home, my heart pounding, consumed with absolute fear that I would receive nothing and finally be forced to admit the unbearable and unthinkable.

As we went into her reading room, I sat down with my arms crossed. I looked at her and said that I wasn't being closed as a test to her, but rather because I had lost someone very dear and I desperately needed reassurance they were okay.

The first thing she said was that there was a room full of spirits with us but three had stepped forward.

The first, she said, was my grandmother. She immediately said that she knew that wasn't who I was there to see, but that she just wanted to come through to say hello.

"She is saying that you have her feistiness and she loves that. She is laughing, and also said to tell you that you can't cook like her, though."

This made me laugh, as I am very much like my grandmother. But while she had made her living as a cook, cooking is very low on my list of skills.

"Your grandmother is saying something about 'your son with your eyes.'"

I replied that all three of my sons had my eyes.

She grabbed her heart and tears filled her eyes. "Oh my, your son with your eyes is your tragedy." She said she could feel the terrible ache in both our hearts as she sat there holding hers.

I started to cry as well.

"He is right here," she said. "He keeps saying, 'Mom, this wasn't your fault.' He's said it five times. He needs you to know this."

"He says, 'I know people see what I did was wrong, but it was too much for me to live with and it had to be.'"

Through my tears, I replied, "No, I have never thought this was wrong, I watched you struggle and try to stay with us. I don't blame you at all."

Through this woman whom I'd first seen only 10 minutes before, I could honestly share with the other side that I understood my son had lost his life to an illness, and there was no shame or wrongdoing in his death from my perspective.

She went into his description of what it was like to have a mental illness, how the periods of mania were as bad as the depths of the depression, and how he felt completely alone in his battle.

"He says that you think nobody understands, and you feel completely tormented by yourself. It is a feeling of being completely alone."

She spoke extensively of what Eric showed her, the happy childhood playing. But even then, he was hyper. She told me he was indeed bipolar, as suspected but never formally diagnosed, and described how his mind never turned off, how he couldn't sleep at night, that he was over-sensitive and would feel others' pain and in his times of darkness, he was consumed by anger, sadness and negative thoughts.

There were many other messages from Eric, very personal, including me sleeping with his old hoodie that he laughingly said was "just an old rag," or that he called Conner "the smart one" and said that despite completing his pilot training, Conner would one day go back to school.

Debby delivered clear messages from my father as well—that he was a farmer and a hard worker, his huge hands, his love for his family and belief in integrity in all you do, his love of pie and how he enjoyed the drink.

"Make sure you say 'the drink,' not 'a drink,' so she knows it's me!" she quoted him as saying.

She told me that he said I had a harder life than my brothers and that he was sorry he wasn't able to protect me. But that I had always been strong, that he loved to watch me as a little girl because I didn't know my own strength of character then, or even now.

Most importantly to me, though, she said, "He is patting your son on the head and he wants you to know that he has your little boy with him and that he is taking care of him for you."

"Eric," she told me, "wants you to write. He says that the mentally ill need to have hope and there are books you need to write—not just one, but three."

Through Debby, he told me to find my voice again, to sing like I did when they were little, and to know that he would be waiting there for me when it was my time to come, just like Grandpa was there to greet him when he crossed over.

Debby also laughed and added, "I can't believe I am saying this, given what I do. But Eric is saying, 'Enough with the psychics, Mom. Some are real and some aren't, and you know the difference. But it's okay for a special occasion or something.'"

With a "See you soon" and a gesture towards my eyes, Eric promised he would visit me in my dreams. And the reading was over.

That was August 8, 2014—369 days after the most awful day of my life.

8

Rebuilding

"Dear God, I pray that when I am
down that I find it within to come up."
—Eric Schmit

The Pieces Slowly Come Together

The year had indeed been one of overwhelming sorrow, numbness, physical and emotional exhaustion. Somehow, the anniversary meant to me that I now had to find a way to go forward, that this timeframe defined the trajectory of sorrow.

I thought of the music from Eric's funeral and the question from *Arms of Heaven*: do the tears we cry change the way we live?

As a communications professional, I decided I would do this by telling Eric's story and our story. Working in the mental health field was the perfect outlet to do this, in the hope that we could challenge stigma and create understanding and compassion for those who had mental illness and addiction disorders. With the public focused so much in recent times on mental health, working in this field offered unlimited opportunities for me to do just that.

As part of my job, I often filtered media requests. An inquiry came in looking for a family who might be willing to discuss surviving suicide loss and how they talked about it. I replied to the writer, who explained that she was doing a story on suicide and how the dialogue around it had changed, so that people no longer cloaked it in euphemisms but instead spoke to the death with honesty, challenging the stigma associated with this type of loss.

As the article was for *Canadian Living* magazine, she said she was looking for a family in Eastern Canada and one in Western Canada to give it a national perspective. I gave her names in both parts of the country, and said that I was also very open to speaking about our family's loss, and Eric's story as well. Eventually, she decided, instead of the national story, to interview me and Justin. Conner has grieved quietly, vastly different than how Justin and I have, and so he declined sharing his grief publicly.

The writer asked some profound questions. One that stood out was around stigma; had we experienced it in Eric's struggle, in our loss, or was it, she wondered, more a fear of stigma? That was the first time I had heard the concept addressed that way, and it made so much sense.

Did we as a family ever question standing beside Eric during his most difficult battles? Absolutely not. We didn't understand it, but we didn't have to come to a decision to be there for him. We just were. In fact, the closeness and bond of our family simply drew tighter.

Did we hide anything in Eric's passing? No, we spoke openly about how he died and even the challenges he had faced and—we thought—had overcome. We spoke openly about the impact alcohol had on his mental health and how that single element seemed to be the one piece he couldn't manage, despite the negative impact.

But this question opened another one for me: how did Eric feel? He didn't want to have a mental illness. He desperately wanted to be "fixed," as he would say. We knew from reading his journals after he died that his highs or periods of mania were as perplexing and terrifying to him as the lows which would inevitably come. Perhaps it was that desperate search for what he perceived as "normal" that prevented him from reaching out, and instead resulted in him masking the turmoil. These were some of the many questions that we unfortunately would never answer.

But this was the one question that had never been asked previously, or since, and one I frequently reflect on, myself, when discussing stigma and mental illness.

The process was arduous in terms of fact-checking and questions back and forth, and for once I was on the other side of the story—not the storyteller, but the subject. There was apprehension about how this story would be told, and I felt a distinct loss of control, knowing our story was in the hands of someone else.

A week after our first-year anniversary, mental health found a place on the world stage, when the world was rocked by the suicide of beloved comedian Robin Williams at the age of 63. Williams had graced the entertainment world with his gifts of comedic beauty and passion for four decades. His family immediately disclosed that he had taken his life after a long struggle with his mental and physical health and addiction issues, and in that asked for privacy while they mourned.

Williams' death marked an important chapter in the anti-stigma movement, demanding understanding and compassion for those with mental health and addiction challenges. An outpouring of compassion and grief globally underscored a new era in how people were looking at, thinking about, and talking about mental illness.

Within the scope of my job, I did several interviews. One story in particular used Williams' death to highlight suicide statistics, as well as the journeys of those with mental illness and survivors of suicide loss. The reporter addressed that I had just passed the first-year anniversary and we worked through some tough questions. I supplied him with photos of Eric in his many activities, our family and Eric with Kathryn.

Once the interview was completed, I was terrified to watch it. My worry was that, as much as I tried to protect Justin and Conner and speak to my own experiences, not theirs, I may have inadvertently said something that would reopen the wounds for them. I checked repeatedly online for the story, and then went to APEX for a boxing class to take my mind off waiting.

A friend called while I was at the gym to say she had seen the story. As a mother of younger children, she told me that watching the story, she saw the unfolding of a beautiful life. Seeing the loss of Eric and its impact on our family, the message she took away was that if this could happen to him, then it could happen to anyone.

My fear of saying something that hurt instead of helped was unrealized. That was exactly the message I had hoped would come across. If we believed that it was someone else's child, someone else's family, or that people with mental illness were "them" instead of "us," stigma would always continue to dominate the conversation and prevent individuals and families from seeking and accessing the help that was so desperately needed.

Summer faded into fall, and the next big marker was the story in *Canadian Living* appearing in the Thanksgiving edition. Despite the interview and fact-checking process having been completed prior to the summer, the story appeared across Canada in October, Eric's Thanksgiving birthday.

Kate Rae, the journalist, had done a remarkable job in this story, *Lifting the Veil*. It was about Eric, about suicide loss, about removing the stigma, about the difficult journey, complimented with photos. Like the CTV story, it left the lasting message that mental illness wasn't a disease relegated to any demographic, but instead one that could strike anyone at any time.

The article encapsulated the memories and the experience exactly as I had hoped the story would be told. Being a writer myself, I marveled at how accurately she had been able to capture each piece and tell the story with such compassion and empathy, without losing any of the truth, even the harder pieces.

Days Move Onward

Our second Christmas without Eric came in 2014. This year was pronouncedly different than the first. If at first, we didn't know how to navigate this important religious and family holiday, in the second year, we were trying to fill it as best we could—with an empty space in our hearts and at the table.

Unlike the previous year, when we simply survived from moment to moment, this year we knew for sure, despite our familiar sorrow, that we would spend Christmas at home and that we had to make something of the day. The tree was up. We even bought presents. I did my traditional Christmas baking, without the urging from Conner for normalcy.

As I was driving to Calgary one morning, I tried to think of what Eric might want for his brothers for Christmas. Having his bank account still open under my name, I carefully dispensed the money on what I thought would be meaningful to Eric. The thought came to me that if Eric could have anything, it would be the opportunity to speak to his brothers.

I called Debby, the medium that I had seen in August, marking the first-year anniversary. She said to me that I mustn't be on her mailing list, as she had just sent an email to clients, letting them know of her Christmas special—buy one, get one free.

Despite Eric's generosity, he was still always careful with his money, as he wouldn't take anything unless he had earned it. I smiled, thinking Eric had just delivered me double the value for his brothers.

When I went to her house to pick up the gift certificates, my own sadness was profound. The winter thus far was proving difficult. The short days, the snow and the cold seemed to exacerbate the barrenness in my own heart. As much as I was struggling to put on a brave face for Justin and Conner, I had not progressed in my grief. My heart had been shattered, and despite the passing of time, it didn't seem possible that it would ever be whole.

Despite every path I had gone down in search of an answer, and how remarkable the validations I had received, I still struggled with belief in an afterlife. Desperately needing to find some way of continuing connection with my son, I once again sought out a reading as solace for my grief. After all, hadn't Eric said in my last reading that special occasions were allowed?

The messages again were so accurate that I remember leaving there reflecting that unless someone lived inside our home, and even inside our hearts, they couldn't possibly have known some of the private pieces of our shattered beings.

She spoke of many things that brought me some comfort. And for the first time, I found the courage to ask about whether there really was a Heaven.

She told me that he said, "It is called many things, Mom, but yes. It's not like Earth and not like space. There is order, and yet there is none. There is kindness and peace and comfort. There are things I can't share. There is no Garden of Eden, and no Adam and Eve, but there is a safe place for us to be. It's where we reflect on what we have learned. There are so many secrets that I can't tell."

Although a practicing Catholic, I hadn't really delved deeply into the Bible. The Old Testament was filled with questions that I didn't even try to answer, so Eric's revelations really didn't challenge my world view. It was as though the foundation remained the same, but the house itself was undergoing a complete renovation, and I wasn't sure what it was going to look like when it was complete.

But for the most part, Eric's focus in this reading was on my writing and telling his story.

Eric believed in my writing and saw it as a responsibility for me. From the time he was a small superhero, needing me to capture his exploits, not yet able to put a pen to paper to capture these adventures, my hand had been his tool. As he grew, Eric always wanted me to write.

"You're a writer, Mom, write," he used to say to me.

He set up folders on my computer, even going so far as to set up a writing schedule for me. But I resisted. I felt I didn't have anything to say during those times. Eric himself wrote at length, he journaled, weaving the most profound stories with his wisdom and true gift for writing. Often, I was surprised at this depth he had, emotionally and intellectually, for his relative youth. And in that I felt inadequate, my own creative capacity having been stripped after years of corporate communications.

With Eric's death, I knew it was important to tell his story. And it seemed that he certainly wasn't letting me off the hook from the other side.

Initially, I wanted to write about this battle with mental illness and call it *The Fight of His Life*. As tough as he was, and Eric was the toughest, most courageous person I have ever known, the daily struggle his mental illness presented was indeed the fight of, and for, his life.

A hockey tough guy, a mixed martial arts warrior, Eric didn't back down. At his last fight, Justin was in his corner and he cautioned Eric to watch out for his opponent's tough right hook. Eric just looked at him and asked, "What's the worst that he can do? Knock me out?"

Eric's calmness in physical danger was evidence of the strength of character he had developed over the years. His external face was one of not fearlessness, but of courage, of the ability to overcome fear and face what he needed to in a calm, contemplative way.

The challenges he had faced in his early years gave Eric a deep understanding of how to manage physical elements of struggle, of challenge. It was the internal struggle, the one he couldn't manage, that haunted him.

Still Piecing Together the Puzzle

I made arrangements early in 2015 to rent a small villa on the coast of Croatia, near Trogir where I had visited the year before. From this place, I would take the time to complete my writing and editing and do a second pilgrimage to Medjugorje. This would be about a 140—150 kilometre trek from the medieval coastal city of Split, in Croatia, to the mountainous village in Bosnia. The plan was that once I arrived, I would purchase, once again from Eric's bank account, a statue of Our Lady of Medjugorje, and take it home to Kenaston cemetery to honour many things: our Croatian roots in Lovinac, the home our ancestors had found in Canada, our resting place and our eternal home. Even though at this point I still had not found confidence or secured my faith again, the value of roots had become important to me in the days following Eric's death and this seemed to be a way to acknowledge and respect this.

I had searched for the "right" place for my writing retreat, and in the search found a tiny seaside village which looked eerily similar to what Eric had shown me during my past life regression, prior to my first visit. It was here that he had directed me to write, to "take the time, but make the time."

Although I wanted to write Eric's story, and understood that in order for me to find a path out of my own pain there needed to come a day when I would break through my own barriers and begin to collect the thoughts that were ever present in my own psyche, I was at a loss as to how to start this process. In research language, it would be called narrative completion, being able to make sense of the tragedy by weaving the fractured images of the pain into a cohesive narrative—finding a place for the tragedy within my life story.

We have a saying in our family about keeping your word. We call it "keeping your contracts." Eric had continuously badgered me to write, and I often half-heartedly agreed. Now, I believed that I needed to live up to this belief Eric had in me throughout his entire life—that my destiny involved writing. This commitment to my deceased son drove me more than any academic need to capture the loss and find meaning. But as much as I wanted to, somehow, I couldn't find the courage to begin.

In my last reading with Debby, she told me that Eric was showing her a suitcase and said he was going on a trip with me, laughing. And Conner was coming too. She said she could see us laughing and drinking wine, which she questioned, as she knew I wasn't one to drink.

She shared that we would hear church bells ringing in the distance.

Eric, she told me, promised that this would be a beautifully challenging trip, but that it was here where I would finally find the peace I needed.

No Choice But to Begin

Easter of 2015 offered me a framework for that beginning. In Catholicism, the period of Lent had traditionally been viewed as one of symbolically walking with Jesus through the last 40 days of his life, through common sorrow. Often individuals carried out their Lenten journey by giving something up—such as coffee or sweets. For the past few years, I had adapted my own Lenten journey to instead try to honour the life of Christ by focusing on the goodness and love he spoke of, rather than the sorrow of his final days. I decided that for this Lent, it was time for me to begin writing, to keep my contract with Eric.

Many times, as he had encouraged me to write, I questioned Eric about the what and the how. He had told me not to worry about it, just to write every day for 15 minutes and the meaning would come. The structure provided by Lent offered me a way to start. So, for 15 minutes every day, I sat and wrote. This gave me time to reflect, to collect my thoughts, but also to be a promise-keeper and keep my contract with Eric. It seemed that just as he had done in his childhood, standing there in his little Bat suit, directing me to write about his super-hero exploits, Eric continued to be my inspiration, and I was destined to once again be the hand that captured his stories.

The Addiction of Escape

From January to August, I was completely immersed in work. And then, at the end of my long work day, I came home and trained at the gym, or focused on the gym's business. Although initially the silent investor, I had since taken over complete ownership.

I lived in a state of exhaustion, physically and emotionally, as I relentlessly sought escape from the reality I struggled to face in my heart. When night came, I continued to take sleeping pills as my other escape. Despite the depth of my professional understanding of the journey of grief, I had not yet accepted that I was not coping. I was running from the horrible truth I still could not face. As a mother, I had believed I could cope with anything life threw my way, as long as I had my three sons with me to face it. I had never been prepared to face life without one of them.

There was one thing that I knew from my research and thought about often—the concept of time and how it changed in trauma and loss. The moment I learned of Eric's death, time as I understood it lost all meaning. I literally felt as though my world had stopped, and yet I was perplexed by how the rest of the world continued to move.

As days moved into weeks, then months, I still struggled with time. I had to look outside to know what season it was or look at a calendar to know the month. Grief does this, I now know. Because even though time passes, the feelings and emotions stay the same and we remain locked in that time and place where life changed, regardless of the passage of time external to us.

About that time, Kathryn finished her college program and her parents were in Lethbridge for the graduation. I remember the mixed feelings that I had that first September, seeing her off to school, and the enthusiastic students all starting on their life journeys. Despite my happiness for them, these were all reminders that my own son would not be leaving for college—not now, not ever. He wouldn't enjoy school life, or the challenges of studies and the friendships he would make. All of these experiences, all of this hope, all of this life, left when Eric left.

As Kathryn graduated, it seemed so hard to believe that the time had passed as quickly as it had. My joy for her and her family was a reminder of how differently our lives had played out over the last two years.

Her mother Margaret posted a few pictures on Facebook. I saw this and commented that it seemed just like yesterday that we had seen her off. A few moments later, Margaret sent me a personal text message from the ceremony.

"As we sat here waiting, *Be Still* came on," she said. "Eric is here with us."

Although it might seem to be a coincidence to others, this song by The Fray is hardly mainstream. I had never even heard of it prior to his passing, but when Eric died, I listened to it endlessly, looping the song, listening and re-listening.

"Be still and know that I'm with you, be still and know that I am here."

I replied to Margaret that although it was a sad marker for me, that message brought tears of joy as well. She replied that David worried sharing it would make me cry. But I was so glad she did. That one more reminder, chipping away at my wall of resistance, that life did exist beyond what we could see.

It seemed impossible that we could be approaching the second anniversary of his death. I found it hard to comprehend that to the rest of the world, two years, 730 days, was a very long time. Yet to my mother's broken heart, if I stood still long enough to allow the thoughts to find their way into my being, the emotions they carried with them were as real as in the immediate aftermath of his death, and I would find myself searching for somewhere to flee.

I understood this flight response to my grief. It was how I had coped for almost two years. I thought about Eric, and the writings his brothers had found on his phone.

Fear is nothing. Fear is but a reaction to the past or antici-pation of future pain. In the presence of fear, one can only flee, freeze or fight. In flight, one can only be chased for so long; when frozen, one is already doomed; and in fight, one is made to hurt or be hurt.

It seemed I had been chased long enough and it was time for me to find a way to deal with the grief that I ran from. In the immediacy of Eric's death, I had accessed professional grief counselling through my workplace. Although I found it helpful, in my numbed state, my inability to process made it simply a requirement, based on a checklist developed by the outside world. I realized it was time for something more.

At work, our Director of Client Services checked in on me. She asked me if I felt like if I let go of my grief, I would be letting go of all I had left of Eric. I replied to her that this really was my greatest fear—as illogical as it really was. When she explained to me that this was one of the most common thought processes that accompanies complex grief, it made sense to me.

Even with this understanding of "Why?" I still didn't know the "How?" of finding the courage to let go of my grief and keep Eric close. Every moment, although present in this world, I was still trapped in the missing of his physical presence.

The next morning, I happened to be speaking to Wayne McNeil, Sheldon Kennedy's business partner, about work, but at the end, Wayne asked how I was doing. I always answer honestly when questions about my wellness are posed and admitted that I was struggling, and told him about the conversation about clinging to grief seeing it as all we have left of our loved one.

"I can't say I've experienced anything like the loss of a child," Wayne said. "But what if you gave yourself permission for a few minutes at a time, to just let it go? And then if you find yourself forgetting Eric, it's right there for you to grab onto again."

Those two insights were what I needed to make the transition from being consumed by my loss to being able to let it go for a few moments. Although it was still there, this was the first time I was psychologically able to make that choice to release the pain, even momentarily.

Hey Ma, I'm home!

Like the first anniversary of Eric's death, the second anniversary in 2015 was filled with apprehension. It was different, however, more predictable. The first year, I had no idea what to expect, and I was filled with terror in those days that preceded the anniversary date. This year, my heart ached in sadness, and I wondered, as the heaviness sat on my heart, if there was a deeper intuitive knowledge that would have made me sad even if I didn't have a calendar to tell me that two years had passed in the blink of an eye.

I wanted to go home to Saskatchewan, but knew it couldn't be on the anniversary of his death. Instead, I decided to go the week before. I had a dual purpose for going, though. Bringing the statue of Our Lady home to Kenaston required approval of not only St. Andrew's Church, but also the diocese. The cemetery committee bought into the idea wholeheartedly—especially Gerard Zdunich, who headed up the committee for the parish.

Gerard and I had spoken several times, particularly in June, looking into logistics about the grotto which would house the statue, and how the community could support it. He told me to just worry about bringing the statue home and the grotto coming together would be his to look after. We spoke the day before he and his wife Gina left on holidays, knowing that he would be back in early July for a brief window when I would return to Kenaston to finalize some aspects.

Unfortunately, while on holidays, Gerard became ill, and on returning to Saskatoon was taken straight to St. Paul's Hospital, where the family learned he had pancreatic cancer that had metastasized to the liver. I struggled with whether to reach out to Gerard again before I left for Croatia, or to leave him and his family to deal with this news. I certainly didn't want him worrying about the grotto. However, my mother insisted that it would be important that Gerard knew this was looked after, so I decided to come home and visit him in the hospital.

Friday evening, I left after work for Saskatchewan, arriving after midnight. In the morning, I called his cell phone and his daughter answered, telling me she thought a visit would be a good distraction for him, especially to talk about the grotto, as it was very important to him.

I'm not sure where it came from, but I had a sense that I should give him the rosary from Domigoj, with the Divine Mercy image on it although admittedly I struggled with whether one should re-gift such a precious item.

When we arrived, I was immediately grateful my mother and I had made the trip to Saskatoon for the visit. Gerard was weak and quite ill, but the family was optimistic about his treatment options. In the end, I decided to give him the rosary, as his support was such an important part of having the local part of the project completed and in so doing explained its importance to me. The cancer unexpectedly took him that Wednesday.

When my mother attended the funeral, she saw that blessed rosary in his hands.

Not long after, I reconnected with Robin Davison. When I had met her in Phoenix the year before, I wasn't quite sure about the past life experience initially. But following the experiences in Croatia, where much of what I had seen in the regression had been validated, I now posed an unusual question to her: would she consider coming to Calgary and visiting while also doing Past Life Regressions? I offered my home, both for her to stay and to run the regressions. Surprisingly, she said yes, and early July heralded her arrival.

Robin wanted to offer regressions to myself and Justin for being able to stay in our home.

Mine was interesting and unexpected. In this life, I told her that I was an 11th-century soldier in Spain. I viewed my village from the hilltop above as I brooded over a war I didn't want to go to. I had no father and two smaller siblings, and I was worried about my mother in my absence. In the aftermath of the battle, I stepped across the bodies of soldiers who had not survived. I felt consumed by the senselessness of this, and my heart was heavy.

I found an older soldier, whom I identified as Justin in this life. He was a close friend and had an almost brotherly presence to him. In fact, he called me "little brother" in an endearing way. We walked to the sea and sat on a cliff, watching the water in quiet contemplation. We lay on our backs and stared at the blue sky for awhile, without talking, and then began walking on a trail back to our village. I was devastated by the human cost of war. I went into the stone house and saw my mother and siblings, and, without speaking to them, went behind, into the garden. At the well, in the dark of night, so consumed by the irreconcilable trauma I had experienced in battle, I took the rope from the bucket, put it around my neck, kneeled, and then pushed myself forward into death.

Coming out of the hypnotic trance, I reflected at how closely this experience paralleled Eric's journey through this life. I felt more that I had experienced Eric's story than my own. As with the regression the year before, I didn't understand the meaning. However, given the way I had revisited the places of the memories on my first trip to Croatia, this time I wasn't so skeptical that there was meaning in what I had experienced—I just knew that I would have to wait to find out what that meaning was.

The Second Anniversary

The fact that Eric died on the August long weekend again meant two dreaded remembrances—the Sunday morning of August long weekend, and then August 4, Tuesday. I don't remember much about how Sunday unfolded as I stumbled through the familiar cloud of grief that had descended on me right before the weekend.

But Tuesday morning was very different. I woke in tears and lay in bed, crying, willing myself to rise and forcing myself to participate in the day, regardless of how difficult it was going to be.

I was slow leaving for work, but I was grateful for a workplace that understood my loss as few other places could. I texted the team that I would be late and focused on getting there. I knew the day would be hard, and likely not productive, but at least participating in the day was better than staying in bed, consumed by my grief.

As I drove the hour-long commute, I periodically broke down. I asked Eric for a sign. In response, I swear, in my heart I heard him say to me, "I'm going to send you something incredible, Mom."

This was so strong that I replied out loud, "Okay, Eric, send me something incredible."

My phone had been going off over the entire weekend with calls, text messages and Facebook messages from the many caring friends that were part of my life. The next message wasn't one I was prepared for, though. It was from Robb Nash. I hadn't heard from him in several months.

"Sending you tons of love today, Joy!"

"How strange," I reflected. I wasn't aware that Robb knew the anniversary of Eric's passing. I replied asking if he knew it was the date or his uncanny gift—hearkening back to the Mother's Day he had unexpectedly reached out to me.

"A little of both," he replied. "Maybe read this message when you have some alone time today. I had a dream last night that I was in a music studio in Heaven. (Which made me very happy, by the way . . . To know that there are music studios in Heaven, ha ha.) Anyways, a young man came into the studio and asked me if I could write a song with him and give it to his mom. I said sure. He told me the title and I got chills. It was called *Walking with My Mom Across Earth*. It was beautiful. He wanted me to let you know that he is really enjoying walking with you every day . . . everywhere! The peace on his face as he sang about specific memories of walking with you (even in the last couple months) was so amazing to see. He was showing me pics of the two of you walking and laughing. That's one of his favourite things . . . to see you smile and laugh. The dream was more like a memory than a dream. And I hope this text wasn't too much for you . . . but when I woke up and looked at my calendar and saw that it was the anniversary . . . I knew I was meant to share it with you today! Love you, Joy!"

I couldn't believe it. Once again, out loud, I said, "That wasn't just incredible, Eric, that was really fuckin' incredible!"

The passing of the long weekend left me with less than two weeks to prepare for the trip to Croatia, the pilgrimage and the writing time following it. This also meant two weeks compressed in preparing my work environment for my absence, the middle of the month and month end for the gym, physically training for the pilgrimage and ensuring things were looked after at home. The days were filled and I didn't really have time to reflect on my next adventure.

Croatia Again

When I was in Saskatoon the last weekend in July, I saw my cousin Lynne. Even though Lynne was the Member of Parliament for Blackstrap for 16 years, and part of Stephen Harper's Cabinet, she had been challenged for her constituency's Conservative nomination in the run-up to the 2015 election and defeated. Since she was no longer a candidate, she made the decision to join me for a short period in Croatia for my second Medjugorje pilgrimage, adding it would do her well to be away, if even for a short time. She would fly in and meet me in the coastal

Croatian city of Split, we would do the pilgrimage and she would fly back to Canada while I remained to write at the seaside village I'd found months before.

Despite the journey and what it had meant, facing my pain, I was to learn was not a magic formula for healing. What I had done was simply opened the door and found a place to start. The reality I was beginning to comprehend, as shared with other survivors of traumatic loss, it that you learn and you cope, and you go forward. But you don't really heal. In research terms this would be integrating the experience into your life story.

I called Sheldon the week before I left to ensure I had a chance to talk to him about my book and about him being included in it. Although we are far from close friends, the support and guidance he provided has been instrumental in moving myself through the various paths and pitfalls of my grief. I didn't want to exploit that friendship, nor did I want to have anyone included feel uncomfortable with the backroads of my spiritual journey—the less than mainstream journey through the world of the unknown and often unspoken of psychics and regressions.

I over-explained in my chaotic overly analytical way about the research, being my own case study in narrative completion and post-traumatic growth, and my search for God. Sheldon just looked at me and said "I don't know about any of that other stuff you're talking about. But for what spirituality means to me—it's simple Joy. Every morning I pray to God to give me the strength for today."

Justin and Conner were thrilled when they learnt that Lynne would be joining me. They thought that I would be landing in Croatia—a country that had been at war in both their lifetimes—and walking into the unknown in my quest to find meaning in the loss.

They prepared me as best they could, Justin training me, and sorting out my hiking backpack, sleeping bag and supplies. Conner and his girlfriend Bre also decided to join me on the trip to Croatia.

We arrived late in the afternoon and found our way to the rental villa in the tiny seaside village of Seget Vranjica, images of which reflected the place I had seen in the past life regression. As we sat in the quiet on the patio, sharing a bottle of wine, I was surprised to hear church bells ringing in the distance, and I thought about the reading I had had several months before where Debby had spoken of this trip and the peaceful sound of church bells tolling.

The following morning, we drove to Lovinac to pick up Zeljka, the doctor's wife, from our first trip. She would be leading the pilgrimage and picking her up offered the opportunity to show Conner a few of the family places, including the original farm my grandfather had left in the early 1900s and the cemetery where our ancestors rested.

At the farm, nestled below Budoc Rok, the woman remembered me from my visit the year previously. Her son was at the farm this time and was able, in his limited English, to explain to Conner, Bre and I where the original house was, the next house and the next—the one he had been born in. The house that now existed on the farm was 20 years old. I suspected that they likely rebuilt their home after the war when they could come back to the village, or what was left of it. Lovinac was a Croatian stronghold and much of the village was destroyed during the latest war. Residents had been forced to leave their homes and all their belongings, but they came back to the devastation, to begin the rebuilding process.

There was one final incredible moment as we made our way to the car. Zeljka was still translating as the old woman sought to understand the full connection we had. We both understood that my grandfather Marko (Mike in Canada) was where the familial ties to the farm lay. However, I also said Ika (Eva in Canada) Brkich was my grandmother. Her eyes lit up as she suddenly connected this name to the packages that came from Canada. She said through her tears "the packages your grandmother sent kept us going during the lean years of communism when we had nothing."

This was one of the few things I remembered about my grandmother, how her gratitude for her new home in Canada was expressed in the packages she would send back to the Old Country.

When she had been sent to Canada to marry my grandfather, it had been because she was an orphan girl and the families there, in their poverty, couldn't take care of her. She had been offered as a bride to this man from the village and a home in the new land. Times were difficult; the hard-working immigrant couple raised 11 children, two others lost in infancy, before he was diagnosed with cancer, dying at 62 years of age, leaving her in this new land, unfamiliar with the language and with an entire family to care for and a farm to run. Despite these hardships, it was still a better life than what she had left behind. And she had a deep sense of responsibility for those still in Lovinac. That this woman remembered my grandmother's kindness as sustaining them through those lean, harsh years was so powerful to both of us.

We went back into the village of Lovinac early and loaded the rented car up with bags so that Zeljka and her son, the young priest Domigoj, could travel back to Split with us. About an hour into the drive, Domigoj asked if we could stop at a church where his spiritual advisor was. The priest he had hoped would entertain us was well-known throughout this area of Europe and there was, we were told, a waiting list of more than 800 people hoping to see him and benefit from his prayers.

The priest was not able to see us, but another did and he offered special prayers for our upcoming pilgrimage. It was quickly evident the pureness of the faith of the Croatian people we were going with was different than the faith that I lived in North America. It had been several years since I had made a confession, but I wasn't going to be able to get out of it at this little country church. Unable to tell a lie, I spoke to him about my fractured faith and search for meaning in the loss of my son.

Obviously troubled by how far my faith deviated from Catholic tradition, the priest spent a few hours in prayer with me and for me.

At one point, he looked at the chain around my neck and asked if it held a cross. I held it up and explained that no, it held the ashes of my deceased son. This was the final straw for this priest. He sat upright, looked me in the eyes and told me that I had troubles with possessiveness, and that I needed to understand that Eric was God's son before he was mine.

The experience was so vastly different from anything I'd experienced throughout this process of examination of faith. In North America, the Catholic priests and churches I had visited had been far gentler in their approach to my maternal grief. As had the first priests I had met the year before in Dubrovnik. I had not felt judged, but supported.

This time, although grateful for the experience, while feeling supported, I couldn't reconcile that the pieces which gave me peace in my search for meaning were the very things this priest found so worrisome in a follower of the Catholic faith.

That night, after we arrived back at the villa, conversations with Conner, Bre and Lynne who had flown in earlier that day, helped me to reframe the day's events so that I was in a place where I didn't feel such guilt and shame for questioning the doctrines of my faith, the meaning in my loss, and not blindly accepting a dogmatic world view that I couldn't find comfort in.

While I appreciated his faith, I questioned how could he understand what it was like for a mother to face the loss of a child she had once carried inside her, felt grow, brought to life and cared for every day of his life? How could he judge my journey or lack of faith?

I found comfort in the late-night conversation back at our lodgings with my family, which helped reconcile the experience in the church which had left me deeply troubled.

The Journey Continues

The next day marked the start of our pilgrimage. For the first time, the immensity of what we were about to undertake hit me. I experienced momentary panic and wondered how I could abandon the pilgrimage and yet save face. I also knew in my heart that this pilgrimage was somehow instrumental in my healing journey and there was no turning back. I knew I had to find a way to stop the running, and to find peace with this loss so that I could learn to live again, instead of the numbing state of exhaustion that had become my existence.

There were five of us in total, Lynne, Zeljka, and two Croatian women Nvenka and Vezna that would make the pilgrimage. Before we left shortly before midnight, I was able to connect momentarily with Conner. He had driven to Dubrovnik with Bre, and I was happy to learn they had made it safely back at the villa. I could start the trek without that additional worry hanging over my head.

We began the long walk through the darkness to cross the first mountain range. At about 7 a.m., we came to a churchyard with an adjacent cemetery on the outskirts of the village of Bisko. The cemeteries in Croatia were representative of a strong faith and love of family. The tombs were not only spectacular but well cared for. We laid our sleeping bags out on the cement path outside one of the outbuildings. As I closed my eyes in exhaustion, I saw Eric's beautiful face float before me, blonde curls circling his face, smiling. I wondered whether it was my imagination or real. And then I was asleep.

As we walked, we crossed an intersection of two roads and I noticed what appeared to be an abandoned, vaguely militaristic housing complex to the east. Vezna ran ahead to one of the homes and a man appeared in the doorway, then came out to welcome us all and invite us into their garden for "*kava*," or coffee. Zeljka explained that he had been on a previous pilgrimage with her and Vezna. He and his wife were Bosnian refugees and had been relocated during the war.

After some drinks and a short visit, Zeljko walked with us to the main highway, where we once again continued our walk. As he stood there behind us, his big hand waving, it was one of the first moments where I really began to consider the immensity of loss and the courage to rebuild that the people we encountered had displayed. The people, not just there, but everywhere we journeyed, had lost everything in a war that had a country come apart from the inside out. These people in particular had come as refugees into an impoverished country, needing only a place to call home. And from that they survived. I couldn't help but think about how they had little outside of their faith and wondered if it had always guided and sustained them or whether they too had gone through their own darkness to find their way back.

We had walked 21 out of the past 24 hours when we finally turned into a churchyard in Cista Vrjanka, one of three small villages which made up the "three sisters", and about five kilometres before Cista Provo. The churchyard was adjacent to two large dwellings where sisters and priests lived. Zeljka and Lynne went to the front door and were greeted by one of the nuns, who gave us permission to sleep in the yard. Exhausted, Lynne and I rolled out our mats and sleeping bags, and within moments were fast asleep under the massive pine trees that separated the houses from the road.

The plan had been to only sleep until about 3 a.m. and continue. Being susceptible to migraine headaches during periods of fatigue or exertion, and rapid barometric pressure changes when the weather rapidly changes; as a storm rolled in, so too did a headache. Laying on the ground beneath the church bells, which tolled with every hour, I worried that I would not be able to complete the pilgrimage. Continuing simply would not be an option, and I planned how to contact Conner and Bre to come and get me in the morning.

As the church bells tolled for 3 a.m., I prayed in earnest. For the first time since Eric had died, I was praying to a God I believed in, not that I hoped was there. I prayed that my headache would leave so that I could continue for the rest of the pilgrimage with these amazing women who surrounded me. As the clouds left and the sun slowly rose, I closed my eyes and slept.

I didn't awake until 5:30 a.m., when the rest of the crew bustled. There was some concern about us being behind schedule, but I articulated that had we not overslept, I would not have been able to continue, and that I had prayed to stay on the pilgrimage. I told them I believed it was an answer to that early morning prayer.

As I lay there, I grabbed the medal around my neck which contained Eric's ashes and realized the message that had come from Robb Nash just two short weeks before "walking with my mom across Earth" was unfolding. I held it, as I often did, and this time, instead of questioning where he was, whispered a silent prayer of thanks that my boy was accompanying me on the journey.

That stop was the only real rest we took throughout the trek.

As we met others along the way, Lynne began to ask in Croatian, "How far to Medjugorje?"

We also noticed that while there were directional signs, they lacked numerical distance markers. As North Americans, we struggled with this. I would message Conner, give him a location and ask him to look it up to give us a sense of what we were doing and what kind of progress we were making. I would also message him and Justin with periodic updates so that they could let Lynne's daughters in Canada know where we were and that we were surviving.

What was fascinating was that the people were of such faith that as we walked, we were greeted by honking horns and waves, and questions as to where we were going. If they stopped to chat, we were left with wishes for a safe journey.

Near midnight, we finally reached the border between Croatia and Bosnia-Herzegovina. My feet could barely carry me at this point, and Nvenka took me first to the border crossing so that I could get across and rest my feet for a few minutes. The crossing was confusing and intimidating. A young Croat guard was quite helpful and as Nvenka handed me over to him, he walked with me through a Bosnian checkpoint and a police station. He also showed me where I could sit on the ground for a few moments while the rest of the crew waited for Zeljka to catch up. I felt scared being separated from my companions by this border, even if it was only for a few minutes.

The energy of the area was cold, and for the first time in our travels, I felt concern about the wisdom of the journey and our own personal safety. In the few moments I had, and with little battery life left on my phone, I called my mother to let her know our exact location.

We unrolled our bags, and like the previous night (which now seemed like an eternity ago), we kept them close together for sleep. This time, we agreed to awaken in a few hours and be on the road by 2:30 a.m. We were told that Medjugorje was 50 or 60 kilometres from the border. As it wasn't as mountainous as the days before, we planned to make it by evening.

As the sun rose, we arrived in Grude, a relatively large, more cosmopolitan, centre than what we had so far seen. We stopped at a market at the top of one of the hill crests on our way out of town. A policeman pulled over and explained to us that there was a short cut to Medjugorje as we approached the south side of the town.

Following his instructions, we found ourselves on a narrow twisting road through the hillsides. It was a major road for locals through to Medjugorje, but narrow, and the pavement was cracked and old. We knew it was 34 kilometres from this corner to our destination; this route shaved 10 kilometres off of the original path. But ultimately, it wasn't the distance that made this route the right choice for us. In these final kilometres of the pilgrimage, my own journey began to come together.

So much of the path was reminiscent of my childhood in rural Saskatchewan, walking the roads to our grandmother's house in the heat of the summer. The people we encountered along the way could have been any of our neighbours or relatives, so strong was the cultural tie between the old country and the new land. And despite being an ocean apart, the landscape wasn't markedly different from the rocky hills east of Kenaston where our families had farmed and continued to do so. The little Bosnian villages we walked through along the path were distinctly similar to those in the Lovinac area, with stone houses, stone fences and centuries of presence.

Lynne was far more gregarious than I, and so each place we walked by, she would ask, "How far to Medjugorje?" which would be greeted with an invitation to stop for water or a visit. Our water bottles never went empty, nor did our bellies.

As we stopped for water, I rubbed my aching feet, taking my shoes off while we rested. I had long since given up wearing my training shoes and instead opted for my Birkenstocks. This way I could keep my feet open and it seemed to help with preventing new blisters. However, my feet were very swollen and sore by this point. Each time I would get up, the first few steps were excruciating. My big toes had swollen beyond recognition within the first day and keeping closed shoes was simply too painful. Nvenka followed my lead and both of us kept our sandals as our main footwear. Lynne had some "toner" shoes, built with cushions on the impact points of the foot. She was the only one of the team who didn't have blisters. Perhaps Vezna didn't either, but she never complained or admitted to any aches and pains. She simply walked quietly with the group.

By now, "How far to Medjugorje?" was greeted in hours. The last two stops had said four hours. Lynne and I had become separated from the other three and stopped at a farm where two lovely English-speaking twin girls invited us in to rest, the girls repeated this answer. Our team caught up to us here, and we all left together, but it was to be the last time we saw each other until after the pilgrimage ended. Lynne, Nvenka and I walked ahead. We were worried about our limited time and wanted to get to Medjugorje to find our contact and get the statue of Our Lady destined to return with us to the cemetery in Kenaston.

By now, we had followed the lead of our Croatian counterparts and, instead of waiting for the invitation for food; we simply grabbed handfuls of grapes or fresh tomatoes from the lush gardens along the road. We had adopted a plan for moving that meant we made more frequent stops to rest our feet and walked along the shady side of the road wherever possible to sustain us. Stopping any longer seemed to raise the specter that we might not start again.

By now, every step was pure agony, but I didn't want to complain, knowing that each of my companions suffered equally. *Step by step*, I would tell myself in between stops. The outside bones of my feet hurt from overcompensating and my hips were experiencing shooting pains.

It was along this road that I turned to Lynne and mentioned how grateful I was that we had taken the shortcut, the back roads. I told her how I always take back roads because that is where you see everything. We agreed that we had experienced the miracle of Medjugorje here on this winding road in the faces and hearts of the people, who simply opened themselves up to us. We weren't the most attractive crew, but no one questioned opening their homes and giving us what they had to make our journey easier.

We wondered how we would have been greeted elsewhere, or more specifically how we would have greeted similar pilgrims in Canada. What we had experienced was so vividly reminiscent of our childhoods and how we were raised. We had both gone so far from that in our own lives, where everything had become planned and rushed.

As I walked, I began to feel there genuinely was something special about this walk in the hills near Medjugorje. I thought about 1981, when the Blessed Mother first appeared to the peasant children tending to the sheep, how unlikely it was that this message would spread, particularly under a Communist regime where Christianity was forbidden. Today, in a world dominated by technology, at times something grabs the population's interest for a fleeting moment and spreads across the globe. But almost 35 years ago, from the impoverished hills of the former Yugoslavia, the spreading of Mary's message to the world was highly improbable. However, her message did spread, and today the messages that came out of the mountainous region continue to be a magnet for millions of pilgrims searching for meaning. Like me.

I also thought about the advice Sheldon had given me as we had a coffee before I left, about how you make a journey like this—one step at a time. Each plodding, pain-filled step, I thought about that.

And I thought about Eric, about how every day was a battle for him. About the parallels that existed between his journey and mine. But it was in the differences, that gave me an option to keep going and him to finally surrender. His pain wasn't an external one that you could pull away and heal, like sore feet. There really was no destination for him to arrive at, just a vague concept of being "fixed" that he desperately prayed would happen.

"Lynne," I said, "I have found what I came for."

As I wrapped up this pilgrimage I had a greater understanding of what Sheldon had been trying to tell me. The path through loss, chaos and pain, and hopefully to a way to find meaning and live with this loss is individual, and in that so too is the understanding of what God means. It is deeply personal and individual.

Did my grief end on the pilgrimage? Not in the least. But now I was now more comfortable in the understanding that this trauma of losing Eric was not something that could be processed and put into a neat little box. This would be a part of who I am; my new identity. Tragedy, trauma, loss changes us forever. Who we were going into that life storm will not be the same person we are when we emerge.

9

A New Kind of Journey

"I'm not too sure about God or Satan, or heaven
and hell. But, if this is my one chance, my only
chance to experience this beautiful life and beautiful
world, I want to make damn sure it's worth it."
—Eric Schmit

Time for Rest

Following my return from Croatia in 2015, I read the
book *The Pilgrimage* by Paulo Coelho and was intrigued
by the story of the Camino de Santiago, the legendary
route pilgrims take through northern Spain and parts of
France. I had heard of The Way, as it's also called, but
I had little interest in doing it, feeling it was too com-
mercialized and popular. I preferred back roads off the
beaten track.

As the days started leading up to the third anniversary of Eric's death, however, the familiar stirring started.
I could feel the usual need to run somewhere to escape
my pain. That feeling came with certain dates—his birthday, special celebrations like Christmas and Mother's

Day—but was most pronounced at the anniversary. I knew it too well, this sense of desperation and a need to escape from myself. Psychology would say this was a stress response—fight, flight or freeze.

Although at this time I had no real understanding of the concept of pilgrimages and what trekking was, somehow what I had experienced the year before as I walked was emerging as a possible solution to escape myself and my pain.

I began researching and learned of an alternate route, the Camino Primitivo, which was the one the King of Asturias had followed when he made his original trek to Santiago de Compostela. At 343 kilometres, the trek was not as long as the better-known Way, but it offered a more remote, removed, and a more challenging experience than the Camino Frances, the one made popular by the movie *The Way* with Emilio Estevez and Martin Sheen. The harder way seemed a metaphor for my life, and so I decided that this would be the appropriate Camino for me to pursue.

With the trip booked for the summer of 2016, I wanted to spend more time with my mom before I headed to Europe, so we decided that I should drive her to British Columbia to see her brother and my aunt. The night before her and I left, I checked in with a new medium I had heard of; Julie Worthington. A friend who lost her son after Eric had recommended her. She said Eric was showing her an airplane and a backpack, and that I was going on a trip. I said yes, I was. She told me he said to pack extra shoelaces and some Glosette's raisins. She told me that he said he was proud of me, that I needed to do more of this for myself and that this would take me completely out of my comfort zone. She said he was showing her me writing in a notebook and taking lots of pictures.

Then she asked if we had recently had flooding in the basement at our house—that Eric was showing her water in the basement. This didn't make sense to me, and so I told her that we had replaced the toilet a few weeks before, that there had been a small leak, and this must be what he was referring to. And then he talked about how proud he was of both of his brothers—Justin and the gym, and Conner and how he had built such good things from the tragedy.

Mom, my niece and I left the following afternoon for BC. As we made our way west, we could see a huge storm to the north and east. Conner phoned me as he drove through it. He said he had never driven in a storm like that before. The following day, he called to let me know the basement had flooded in the storm that had blown through. All three window wells were filled with water and it had entered the home through his and Eric's windows and the family room window. He pumped out the water and borrowed an industrial carpet cleaner from a co-worker to get on top of it before I got home. Although this should have been upsetting, especially given that insurance doesn't cover claims like this, it had the reverse effect on me. The flood, the water in the basement, affirmed for me Eric's ongoing presence. This, after all the messages, seemed to be the tipping point— the one piece of irrefutable proof I needed to believe that Eric was near and still present.

Another Journey of Faith

Before I left however, there was the business of the business which I had neglected for months as an investor. Although the business was good in the evenings we were struggling because we didn't have day time usage and couldn't seem to come up with a day to fill those hours.

We had met with Siksika Health Services in early July, to discuss programming for Indigenous youth from the reserve only kilometres from Strathmore. Knowing I was leaving in a few days, and with no program in place yet, I put together one final email to the team, in the hope we could develop a program that would work for the youth and which would allow us to keep the business open as our financial situation was dismal.

We had a lunch meeting on Monday to finalize details. At the meeting we discussed having the gym and the partnership blessed through a revered elder in the Siksika community. I expected this would have to be done without me as I was leaving in less than two days. But, the people we were meeting with felt it important

I be part of the blessing, and so a few quick phone calls and the ceremony was set for the next afternoon.

The Blackfoot culture is remarkable in many aspects; it is deeply spiritual and the community gentle and welcoming. The blessing of the gym underscored this. It wasn't a simple ceremony as I had anticipated, and van loads of people arrived. There were more than 20 in total, people from the community with a deep vested interest in the success of the partnership; from elders to the leaders to the youth.

The elder doing the blessing set herself up on the mats of the gym and asked me first to come forward. Along with her husband, they together explained how all things in the Blackfoot culture operate in circles and so I would enter the sacred space through that circle. She then asked why we had wanted the blessing of the gym and I answered that I wanted this to be a true partnership, that the lives we touch with the youth and others would bring positive and meaningful connection to everyone who came through the doors of the gym. She facilitated the blessing, including taking an ochre paint to my face, wrists and arms. The entire ceremony was spoken in Blackfoot.

When finished, she said to me because our intentions were pure that our partnership would be successful. She also said that she didn't understand these things, but that sometimes messages come to her from Spirit and that Spirit had asked her to honour me with a Blackfoot name "Natoyii Kittssta Kia Kii" which she explained means "Holy Offering Woman." From now on, this would be my name. I knew that it is a rare honour to be given an Indian name, but she further explained that it is even rarer that this message would come during a different kind of ceremony as we had just participated in. Usually such an honour is delivered in its own special ceremony. She printed the name and helped me to practice saying it. From now on, when meeting with Blackfoot people this would be the name by which I would introduce myself.

It was then Justin's turn to be blessed; a very private conversation between her and the individual. She used the ceremonial paint to bless him as well, and then when finished she pointed to the picture of Eric that hangs at the entrance of the gym. "When you feel weary or overwhelmed, talk to him. He is here and keeps you strong and your gym strong," she said.

Following this, the SN7 youth, a group of leadership youth also present asked for her special blessings as well. It was an incredibly powerful ceremony and very meaningful and I was so glad I had been present for it, even beyond the honour bestowed on me. I did ponder the delivery of my name as she could not have known that both when visiting Medjugorje and now doing the Camino, that I had decided I would carry specific intentions and prayers for loved ones and situations. The children of the program were prayers I would be carrying this particular journey.

Now, it was time for me to continue my journey of faith—or of holy offerings. Later that afternoon, I put together a small bag of crystals or gemstones. The stones were each picked carefully based on what I felt they represented for the person I was praying for. I told each person what stone I had picked, and why it meant so much. They knew I was carrying this with me on The Way.

When people walk the Camino, they are identified as pilgrims by seashells on their backpacks. I had some I had picked with my dear friend Debbie on a beach, years before when we left Australia and which were kept in a bowl in my living room. I took three out to Robin's farm to see if it was possible to drill holes in the fragile shells. We had been close throughout the many years, and especially so since he had flown me to Saskatchewan at Eric's passing.

He was able to do it, first drilling through the smallest and then through the mid-sized one. I loved the colours of the mid-sized one, and so I told him that this was the one I wanted to use. As I packed my bag later that night, I decided to put both shells on the outside, one to identify me as a pilgrim, the second I intended to leave at Santiago de Compostela when I completed the journey.

Justin has a saying: "I think our mother underestimates the complexities of her adventures." Although they worried about me, they also understood that I was on my own healing journey and as I did with them, we could only support and love each other through it. Conner wanted to attach a GPS to me, but we eventually agreed that I would message them each morning with my plan for the day, and each evening when I was safe for the night.

As I landed in Paris, I messaged the boys that I was going to "just take the train to Oviedo," the city in Spain where the pilgrimage started. My "just take the train" was a serious understatement. It turned out to be a grueling 36-hour journey to my starting point.

As I arrived in Oviedo the evening of July 29, I walked straight out of the train station and into the first hotel on the street. It was in a historic old building, and I was given a room with a double bed that took up almost the entire space. Exhausted, I collapsed into bed for my first real sleep in about four days.

The following morning, when I went out on the street, my first realization was that Oviedo was not a small village, like I imagined, but a large city. I didn't have a clue where to even start. And I quickly learned that English was not really spoken in rural Spain. After wandering for blocks, I eventually found my way back to the train station where I met two young Polish brothers, whom I identified as pilgrims because of the shells on their backpacks. As they spoke some English, they were able to get me to the Cathedral in Oviedo, the official starting place for the Primitivo. Here I purchased my official credentials, which were to be stamped along the route as proof when I arrived in Santiago de Compostela that I had indeed walked the original path.

I had a practice from many years ago that was shared with me by a priest, who said when you arrive somewhere, find a church and pray.

"It is the same God that brought you here that now has a plan for you elsewhere," he had told me. And so, to begin this journey I wanted to stop and pray before setting out.

As I wandered through the massive ancient building, I saw a priest and tried to explain that I wanted to say a rosary to start my Camino. In Spain only a few hours, I was already finding that language was going to be an issue. The priest took the rosary, kissed it, blessed me in Spanish and then led me to the sanctuary, where a second priest blessed me again in Spanish, and then led me to the chapel where I could say my rosary. As I knelt to pray, I suddenly felt very close to Eric, and, missing him immensely, was overcome with emotion and broke down sobbing.

When I left the church, I stopped to eat lunch and as I left encountered what I now call the first of my "angels of the Camino." Like those I'd encountered the previous year, these were those individuals who helped me along the way, and each time provided me lessons in trust as I was genuinely vulnerable. Two older women, reminding me of my mother and one of her dearest friends, called out to me and then chased me down. I was trying to follow the sea shells imbedded in the sidewalks, which point The Way, but one grabbed my hand and shook her head "no," and instead together they led me through the city right to the outskirts.

Using her hands to indicate, she helped me understand this was a shortcut, that the official route went around the city and that this was a short cut. This was no small offering on their part. These were women in the 70s and one was obviously recovering from cancer as she was wearing a wig. The shortcut was probably 15 to 20 minutes of walking to the outskirts of the city. I kissed them both and we blessed each other with the sign of the cross. Now I was truly on my way.

As I started on my road, I realized how much I loved being alone and being in nature. The Camino Primitivo offered me both, and I felt a sense of excitement as I followed the path leading into the hills beyond the city.

Over the course of the first day, I had to make about 29 kilometres. I unfortunately wasn't aware that most *peregrinos*, or pilgrims, start early in the morning. Because of this, *albergues*—inns —are filled early and getting a place to sleep is critical. I had started at noon by the time I'd sorted my day out.

There was a man who had passed me a few times on the trail. Domingo, as I later learned his name was, passed me again as we got closer to Grado, the first stop according to my map. He asked—through hand gestures—if

I needed a place to sleep. I said that I did and that I wanted to get to the town of Grado. He decided to walk with me and stay close, a Godsend as evening came.

As we entered the town, my pack was already weighing extremely heavy and night was upon us. We stopped at an alburgue and were told it was completo, or full. This was the story in each place he tried to find lodging for me.

Eventually we found a hostel, however all that was available was a shared room with twin beds. This was going to be my second lesson that first day in trust and moving way out of my comfort zone. This man had stayed and walked with me for about 10 kilometres so I wouldn't be alone during the evening hours in the forest. Although neither of us spoke the other's language, somehow, he understood that I needed help and had decided to take care of me.

I was terrified of spending the night in a hotel room with a stranger, but even more terrified of spending the night outside, my only other option in that moment. Trust it was. I knew I couldn't tell Justin and Conner this piece of my first night on the Camino, but I also knew someone had to know the situation, so I messaged my close friend Lisa. I carefully worded my message to let the boys know I was in and safe for the night.

We went to get something to eat, late. Seafood is a staple of the diet and the woman in the hotel brought a steaming plate of fish soup. I tried in vain to explain that I had a serious allergy to seafood. Lacking comprehension, she understood I didn't want the soup, so she took it away and brought me a plate of fish instead.

A man at the table next to us, also a peregrino, asked in English if he could help. I explained my allergy, and he explained that he was a nurse, and thankfully, he understood immediately the consequences. He put the phrase "soyalergica al pescado y al marisco. Cualquier pesacdo y marisco" into the notes in my phone and chastised me—appropriately—for not having thought to know this phrase as I would need it throughout my travels in Spain. I made a screen capture of his notes so that I could show this picture each time I had to eat so food preparers would understand I had a life-threatening seafood allergy. Again, I was feeling extremely vulnerable, and Justin's words about me and underestimating complexities of my adventures were weighing heavy on my mind, reality slowly settling in of the accuracy of his words.

My night was quiet although there was music and partying in the street which kept me awake—that and the fact a strange man was sleeping in the bed less than two feet away from me! Eventually I slept and the next morning we arose early, beginning my day two at the break of dawn. Through the help of Google translator, Domingo explained that he was doing the trek in just eight days. This meant he would be travelling ahead, however he promised he would get me safely to the next alburgue for the night. As I walked, I wondered who would replace him as my next angel—to keep me safe from myself!

This July morning, the 31st, was the Sunday morning of the August long weekend, the first of two awful days that I would face this week. As we climbed out of the city and into the mountains, a row of beautiful spider webs sparkled in the early morning mist, along the fence. The web took me back three years to the morning I had sat fascinated by the spider webs on our own backyard fence.

"Thank you, Eric," I whispered.

Fran, the English-speaking nurse, whom I'd met the evening before, was there when Domingo helped me check into my albergue for my second night on the Camino. We talked for a while before I went in search of my bed and fell into an exhausted sleep. Early the next morning, Fran and I found a sandwich and coffee and started off together, the first of many days we started this way.

The therapeutic part of my journey was already manifesting itself. Despite physical exhaustion and pain, the walking was helping alleviate the anxiety that typically ate away at me, day or night. Each step I made, I could separate myself from the internal chaos and immerse myself in nature and in the present. My breathing slowed and my thoughts became clearer.

At one point, about three days into the hike, as I stepped out from a forest trail, I stopped in wonder. Here, high into the mountains, as the forest broke, I was above a sea of clouds, with mountain peaks poking through. I stood in awe, feeling as though I was as close to Heaven as I had ever been in my life. I felt, for the first time in years, a connection to the Divine, of being at peace exactly where I was, and gratitude for the opportunity to be there.

That night, Fran and I stayed in a small village at an alburgue called El Ricardo. A common question on the Camino is, "Why do you walk?" with answers as individual as each person you encountered. I explained my reasons to the owner of the alburgue, Rui. Rui, fluent in English, said that he and his wife had lost a baby just recently and she was struggling with depression.

I asked him to take a story to her for me that I thought might help.

It was from a friend of mine, Chief John Moon from the Blood Tribe in southern Alberta, and his brother. He had taken me on a sacred Blackfoot walk with a few others to the Western Butte of the Sweetgrass Hills in Montana. His brother who accompanied us relayed to me the story of how he had experienced the loss of a baby through miscarriage, and then nearly his own life in a car accident weeks later. As he lay unconscious in the hospital, he said he went to what Indigenous people call the Happy Hunting Ground, or what Christians call Heaven. Here he was greeted by his daughter, the baby that he and his wife had lost, and a brother to him and John who had been killed in a car accident. Both told him that it wasn't his time and he had to return, but his daughter added that she had wanted to meet him . . . and that her living sisters and a brother still to be born needed him.

He recovered, and shortly after was surprised to learn his wife was pregnant again. Later, a son was born true to what he had learned while unconscious. He had shared this story with me during one of my darkest periods of despair to give me confidence and hope that Eric was safe and well; to believe that new life follows death. I in turn shared this story with Rui to take to his wife, Yolanda, to perhaps give her that same hope.

Later that day, Rui returned with a fresh rosebud from their flower garden and said his wife had asked him to give it to me. I pressed it in the little book I was using for notetaking.

Rui explained the route we would be entering the following day was called the Hospitales because of the medieval ruins of hospitals from the 9th Century. These ruins told the story of a strategic military presence along the top of the mountain range that was a physical divide between early Christians and Muslims. As told by Rui, to the north, in Asturias, the Christians resided, and to the south they were vulnerable to invasion from the Muslim armies. The mountain top location helped them to fend off encroaching armies.

Although the trek itself was the most challenging of this particular Camino, there were compensations. The road was awash in the beauty of nature, like the herd of wild Spanish horses in the hospital ruins. At twilight, I made my way to our albergue, where I had a quick bite to eat and soaked my aching feet in ice water. Having been separated from Fran for several hours, lost at one point, and out of water at another, this experience taught me that from then on, it wouldn't just be foolish but dangerous to let myself get far from him and the security he provided me.

August 4th arrived, the third anniversary of Eric's death. Our route for this day involved climbing up one side of a mountain, circling a lake and back up the side of another mountain.

Immersed in nature as before, as I walked alone, I reflected that I was doing quite well considering the date and told myself that indeed I was finding the comfort I needed.

As I stopped at a bend in the switch back on one of the trails down the first mountain side, I stopped to check my phone. As I turned it on, I saw two men coming down the trail.

"*Buen Camino*," we smiled and greeted each other with the typical greeting of The Way. As the first walked by, I looked down at my phone, and there was a message from my friend back home, Alwyn.

"I'm with you today, Joy, and I love you," she wrote.

It was my first connection to the actual date from home and people who had experienced the loss with us. As I looked at the phone in my hand, I was powerless to stop the tears running down my face. Now the pain I thought I had somehow put away hit in full force.

Seeing my tears, the pilgrim, who has just greeted me asked what happened, what was wrong? I explained that today was the third anniversary of my son's death and I had received a message from home. He had tears in his eyes and he looked back at me, speechless. Manolo, as I later learned his name was, reached out and touched my arm. I nodded that I was okay, and then he and his friend moved on. For once, Fran was behind instead of ahead of me, and he was well aware of what the day held for me. As I sat there on the side of the trail, sobbing, he caught up, held me for a few moments while I cried, and then onward we went in silence.

That night, we stayed in a little town called Castro, with a population of 51, in an ancient stone house near the outskirts. Everything I had with me was soaked and/or dirty, so while Fran took the laundry down, I retreated to my room for the evening, in my pyjamas, returning messages from the many loved ones back home in Canada.

The next night, we reached Fonsegrada, one of the largest communities we had been to. Here we found many people we had met earlier along the Camino, including Ksenya, a young Russian girl, and Manolo the man from the trail, with his travel companion Paulo.

The Primitivo was not a popular route, so the handful who travelled it crossed paths daily, even if not staying at the same places. There was a sense of our fellow travelers, and always excitement when we connected with someone we hadn't seen for a few days. It was here where Ksenya's travel companion was forced to leave the trail because of a leg injury, and so I invited her to walk with Fran and me. There was an unspoken rule on the Camino that we were all each other's keepers.

Our first evening of the shared way, was in Boente where our alburgue was across from a medieval church. Ksenya and I went over to the church, found a stamp for our passports and went up to the choir loft where we sat and said our quiet prayers. It was here where I found a prayer card to the Apostle Saint James, the individual the Camino honours and whose relics we were walking towards in the tomb at our destination in Santiago de Compostela. Santiago is Spanish for Saint James.

> *O Apostle Saint James, I am here, as thousands of pilgrims have been through the centuries, offering Our Lord the tiredness caused by following the Way of Saint James. I have come here to learn how to walk through the way of Life . . .*

That night as we ate supper, I took out the bag of stones I had brought, and a piece of the one seashell which was now inside it as well, part having been lost along the way. I looked at the stones and remarked to Ksenya that for so long my work had consumed me in trying to make sure that Eric's life, and death, had meaning. That it wasn't in vain. Yet, it wasn't my work that I thought about on the trail or prayed for. Yes, I prayed that his story could serve to help others, but I prayed for the pieces of my life that mattered most, the pieces I had swept to the side in my grief; family, friends, connection, physical and mental health, our business in the gym and the lives we touched. As I sat there contemplating, Ksenya, in turn pulled out her own small red bag, with stones inside. We talked about how we had planned to leave them at Santiago de Compostela with Saint James as our prayer intentions and our cross for The Way.

We arrived as friends in Santiago de Compostela early in the afternoon of Thursday, August 11, 13 days and 343 kilometres from where we had all made our individual starts.

Our final walk to the square where we could see the Cathedral was very different from what I had anticipated. The crowds, the shops and the identical, mass-produced trinkets that spilled from them inside the old town centre all felt somewhat consumeristic and less than the deeply spiritual ending I had anticipated.

The first thing we did was to take our stamped passports as evidence to receive our credentials. There was a wait for the final paperwork, and as we left the building I went to the chapel to finish my rosary. Ksenya joined me in prayer as had been the practice when we stopped in churches along The Way, then as I stayed to finish the rosary she went ahead to meet with the group already gathering to celebrate all our completion that day.

That evening, after supper, Ksenya and I left for the hotel where we were staying. Rui had delivered us a beautiful experience in a hotel near the centre of town in the old medieval section. Fran, the more social of our trio, stayed, celebrated, and then went and got his first tattoo—the seashell representative of the Camino on his foot.

The following morning, Ksenya and I walked Fran to the bus station as he left for home, and then went to meet with Manolo and Paulo, who had since arrived. As we walked Ksenya asked if I wanted to go to the seaside village Finisterre, which translates into "the end of the Earth." The name of the village had come from Roman times where the cape, or headland, just outside town extending into the sea was then believed to be the end of the known world. We both agreed we couldn't leave the Camino without this final step and although too late to continue on foot, decided to take the bus the next day.

That night, Ksenya, Manolo, Paulo and I attempted to attend the special pilgrim's mass held on Friday evenings. We also wanted to see the *botafumeiro*, the closing ceremony used since the Middle Ages to clean the air following the completion of The Way. In this unique ceremony, a giant thurible, or incense burner, was filled with incense and coal, and eight men swung the 1.5 metre-high container throughout the cathedral. Although we arrived early, so had hundreds of others and the cathedral was full. We were not able to attend the sacred ceremony.

However, in a side entrance to the cathedral, there was a shorter lineup to enter the tomb of Saint James—Santiago—the Apostle. Here you could go up, hug a giant statue of the saint and from there enter the tomb where his relics were for a moment of personal prayer. Although not formally part of the mass, you could see inside the cathedral as you made your way through the church along this route. As we stood in line, Ksenya and Paulo stayed behind and hid to watch the ceremony. Manolo and I walked through as part of the lineup. I stopped and prayed at the tomb while he patiently waited for me.

As we waited for Ksenya and Paulo following the mass, we talked about the day on the mountain when we had met. Manolo told me he misunderstood me and thought I had received word that my son had died three days ago, and I had just received the message. He said he didn't often cry, but in the intense energy of the moment was moved to tears as he could feel and experience my heartache.

When we were eventually joined by the rest of the day's pilgrims, we had one drink, wandered through the medieval town square and again Ksenya and I retired early while the rest enjoyed the evening. It was her 30th birthday, so at our hotel, we sat in the terrace garden and had a glass of wine to toast it and our friendship.

Despite the generational gap between me and this much younger woman, our experience had brought us together in friendship.

We were excited about the final stage of our journey the coming morning. Ksenya and I had determined that the nearby coastal village of Finisterre would be the right place to leave the stones which carried our prayers. Somehow, Santiago de Compostela didn't feel right, the sacredness lost in the energy we couldn't feel.

Going to the End of the Earth

Finisterre, the end of the Earth, seemed such a suitable place to finish my pilgrimage.

In my visit there, it was hardly what I had expected, but delightfully so. Here I was able to feel a sense of completion.

The actual Cape Finisterre, where we wanted to go, was more than 2.5 kilometres from the town. We walked towards it along the coastline. When we arrived, we climbed up to a lighthouse overlooking the sea and experienced this final "end of the Earth."

As we walked up the hill, I suddenly thought about Justin and the past life regression where he and I had been 11th-Century soldiers in Spain. I had briefly thought about it when we had originally planned the Camino together, but not since then as I had impulsively decided to go alone. Now, the image of us sitting post-battle on a cliff along the edge of the water, talking, thinking and contemplating the difficulty of what had just transpired came vividly back to me. Did we really sit here together a thousand years and many lifetimes ago, I wondered? Seeing the rugged coastline, the sea, and the rocky path, I believed with certainty that indeed we had.

We left the lighthouse and walked further up the rugged coast, to where we sat along a cliff at the ocean's edge for several minutes. The water raged against the rocks, the mist hung in the air and I knew I was now *completo*. For the first time in over three years, I felt a sense of genuine peace that wrapped itself around my entire being. This journey had indeed brought me where I needed to be.

There, at the marker which read 0.0 kilometres—the journey's end—Ksenya and I took the stones that we had carried, representing our lives, our sorrows, our worries and prayers for ourselves and our loved ones, and we walked a few hundred metres back to a beautiful bay that we had seen as we started upward. Here, I stepped into the sea, kissed the handful of stones and the broken shell that I had carried in prayer and offering for my loved ones and threw them one by one into the ocean. My bare feet on the stones felt the sea waters rush in towards me, circle around the bottoms of my legs and feet, and then back to the ocean, washing all that I had brought away.

0.0 kilometres. An ending. A beginning.

Conclusion

An Ending, A Beginning

"Give in. Give out. Give everything you've got.
Life, death; we all die. Why worry?"
—Eric Schmit

I had spent three long years looking for Eric, proof that his life mattered and lived on, and searching for firm answers to rebuild my faith around, to understand the mystery that had plagued me since Eric left. What is our purpose here? And where do we go when we die?

I still had no irrefutable proof.

What I did find on my journeys, though, was the faith, hope and love that had been stolen from me in his death. In my search, I found comfort in a new belief that there was a higher purpose to all of this, but a purpose we didn't understand and never would, until we ourselves returned to that home we'd been promised.

The new faith I have come to believe in does not resemble my traditional faith, although it is probably stronger for having been tested as it was. I am a

Christian, I identify as a Catholic, but I've changed in how that guides me. I respect not only my own faith, but each faith which I have been exposed to, believing in the "oneness" that defines the Abrahamic traditions, that we all pray to and worship the same God, the Divine by a different name to different peoples. The fact that all cultural experiences of faith espouse similar messages, similar values and similar ways of telling the story of the world we can't see solidifies that belief for me.

I have learned that we have five senses we trust: sight, smell, touch, taste and sound, but also another sixth sense that we don't really acknowledge. This is one that connects us to the Divine and to the something more, which in some way does answer that question I have been asking. I implicitly trust this additional sense, call it intuition or what you will. It is as real to me as each of the other senses I have relied upon my entire life.

I learned through the afterlife communications I've received from Eric that our loved ones are close and we simply must be aware to hear them. Using any and all of these six senses, we can find them.

I think about Finisterre, and how, with our knowledge today, it seems so limiting to have once believed the Earth was flat and it ended off a cape in Spain. Yet only 500 years ago, with the limited knowledge and worldview at their disposal, that perspective did make sense. Perhaps, like the ancient Romans, someday our worldview of death will be changed. We will have more understanding of what there is beyond our limited knowledge of life, and life beyond this life, making the worldview we now have limited and ancient.

I am no longer running from the pain of my life journey, in particular the loss of my beautiful son Eric. There will always be times that this hurts, and I expect this will be true until my own days come to their end. But I am now familiar with my response and what I need to do to get through those times. It is my story. I embrace it. It is who I am.

I face the realization that while grief doesn't end, it does change. This sorrow, I now understand, does not represent a lack of faith, but the price of love.

Time is a linear concept used to mark minutes, hours and days. But it cannot and never will be able to capture the journeys of the soul we at times face in our lives. Those experiences have a timeframe of their own.

I no longer feel I must let go of my grief according to some external map of the path through loss, created by someone else. The map I created is mine and only mine.

I've literally gone to the end of the Earth in search of all I had I lost when Eric left this physical life. In chasing him to Heaven's door, as he walked with me across Earth, I found what I needed to go on again. I searched for God, and it was in looking deep inside myself, my own soul, that I found Him, the God of my understanding.

My story, my own narrative completion, woven together with the fractured parts of my being—taken from me when my son died, now viewed through the lens of my own understanding—has new meaning. The story of Eric's life. The story of my life. And the story of our story. In my own words. It's simply the story of love that cannot and does not die.

I love you, Eric. I always have, and I always will.

—Momma

About the Author

V. JOY PAVELICH holds a Master of Arts degree in Professional Communications from Royal Roads University. Her Master's research addressed the importance of sharing stories as a tool to move past the damaging impact of trauma. When she lost her 20-year-old son Eric Schmit to suicide in August, 2013, Joy transferred her communications skills into supporting mental health awareness, advocacy and action.

Joy currently works on a national level in a role supporting youth mental health through program delivery and strategy. She has served on the Mental Health Commission of Canada's National Advisory Council for the Mental Health of Emerging Adults, the advisory panel of MoBros (a Movember funded research project to develop a national men's depression screening tool), and was featured in *Canadian Living* magazine, sharing their family story of coping with extreme trauma and loss. She was also profiled in the Calgary-based Home of the Brave initiative, for her work in mental health awareness. She currently resides near Calgary, Alberta, where her sons Justin and Conner remain close.

Rainbow Ridge Books publishes spiritual, metaphysical, and self-help titles, and is distributed by Square One Publishers in Garden City Park, New York.

To contact authors and editors, peruse our titles, and see submission guidelines, please visit our website at www.rainbowridgebooks.com.

For orders and catalogs, please call toll-free: (877) 900-BOOK.